Art of the People

PUBLIC ART

IN THE CITY OF LAFAYETTE, LOUISIANA

BY JEREMY C. BROUSSARD

PHOTOGRAPHY BY TRAVIS GAUTHIER

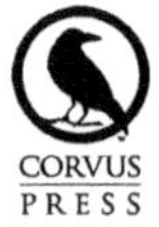

Published by Corvus Press
PO Box 2402, Lafayette, LA 70502
www.corvuspress.net

Written by Jeremy C. Broussard
Photography ©2016 by Travis Gauthier
Layout Design by Elizabeth Bell
Edited by Jessica Moreau

ISBN-13: 978-0-9829239-6-2
Printed in the United States using sustainable forestry methods.

TABLE OF CONTENTS

Introduction

Common occurrences rarely achieve common mention. Sometimes things aren't often noticed . . . not because they are not present . . . rather because they are practically ubiquitous. Such is the case with creativity in Lafayette, Louisiana.

GUMBO — that classic Cajun-Creole dish — would be a fitting example of this cultural phenomena. This cross between a soup and a stew epitomizes the never-ending creativity of the region. First, the dish wouldn't exist without a blend of cultures. African slaves brought okra, an African plant that grew well in South Louisiana's subtropical climate. They called the plant "quingombo" and made a stew with the vegetable that laid a foundation for today's recipe. Cajuns raised livestock and added smoked sausage and chicken to the dish. German immigrants introduced efficient methods for growing rice that rapidly became a staple ingredient in local cuisine and formed the "filler" in the modern recipe. Additional influences from Spanish and Native American residents saw the introduction of various local spices and vegetables such as filé (ground sassafras) and peppers. Without this mix of people the dish simply would not exist. Neither would the diversity and ecclectic nature of this community.

Yet no one owns gumbo. And, at the same time, everyone takes ownership of it. It's a perfect reflection of a community shaped by a people's ability to accept and adapt . . . and create. This one dish inspires and embraces generations of ethnicities.

Just like gumbo, no person or group owns Lafayette's culture yet all of its people take ownership of it.

That's the spirit that lives in this place. It's a spirit of constant acceptance and unending adaptation. They "make do" and "pass a good time," French-derived phrases that illuminate the ideals of a culture that accepts what is given to them and builds something entertaining and creative from what's available.

That constant acceptance and adaptation is so commonplace in Lafayette that it's become expected; the norm. And it seems as though it always has been. As famed muralist and Lafayette native Robert Dafford explains, "There are so many artists here because it's so nurturing. Cajuns are creative people . . . if you couldn't make it, you didn't have it." So they made it. And they accepted that they would always make it. And creativity became a way of life.

Today the once-necessary creative works have become art forms in their own right. Nearly every resident can tell you their favorite local band, style of gumbo, type of boudin (a sausage made with rice and pork), seasonal festival, trending restaurant, weekend activity and more. This place, this space and these people embody a passion for things that elevate the simple to sublime. A dish of rice. A violin. An old house. A town square. It's celebrated and elevated to new meaning.

And such was the case for more than a hundred years. A quiet, happy community — content with itself — relished privately in its own good fortune. But its creativity couldn't be contained forever. Artists branched out. Others noticed the distinct qualities of the region and settled into the culture. The community was a hidden gem no longer. And what was once the hidden passion of a private people became a public and open expression.

And the art that mirrored this lifestyle soon followed. And now the art teaches, reminds and tells us stories about the city and the region. It points out the beauty we may have missed or simply taken for granted.

The city has found the ability to publicly express itself in a creative way. Through art, the city announces to the state, nation and world in a very public manner that this space is unlike all others.

This book bears witness to a compelling catharsis, an uncontrollable release decades in the making. Within each public work of art lies both the roots of an always constantly creative community and the newness of that expression. It's as if the city is ready to shout or even come out wearing the clothes it had only worn privately yet always hoped to wear for the big dance.

And in Lafayette, *the music is just beginning to play.*

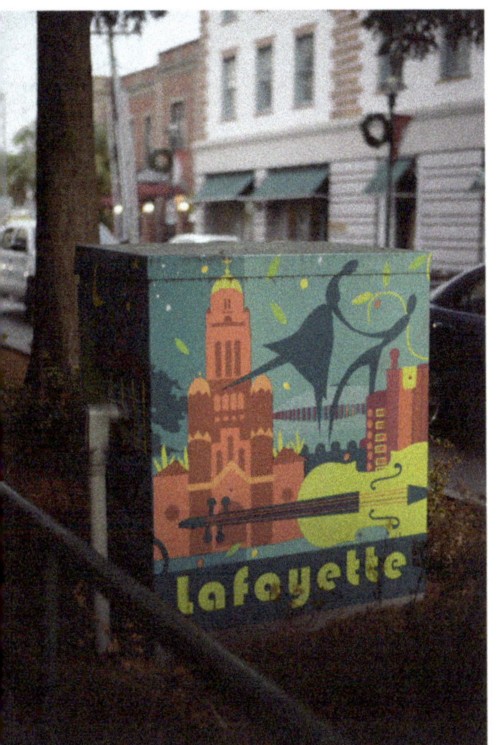

Creativity Everywhere

Lafayette's centuries-old creative energy finds itself channeled through a range of expected and unexpected public art. For example, while you may expect a federal courthouse to feature symbols of U.S. justice, the blindfolded faces[14] holding "watch" at its front steps have no head above the eyebrows.[15] While every city has electrical boxes on nearly every corner, Lafayette joins cities such as San Diego and Calgary by having artists consider the boxes an impromptu canvas and a means of beautifying the space.[16]

"Utility boxes provide artists with an opportunity but also make the space seem more valuable," said University of Louisiana-Lafayette Art Museum[17] Director LouAnne Greenwald. She highlights another unexpected movement: Digital billboards. "More and more they're going up around town and, many times, they commit to supporting public art in one form or another."

An extension of that inspiration can be found in Lafayette's downtown benches. **"Why should benches be plain?"** wondered Downtown Development Authority's Kate Durio. She spearheaded a campaign that continues to involve local artists in painting downtown benches in new and creative ways.

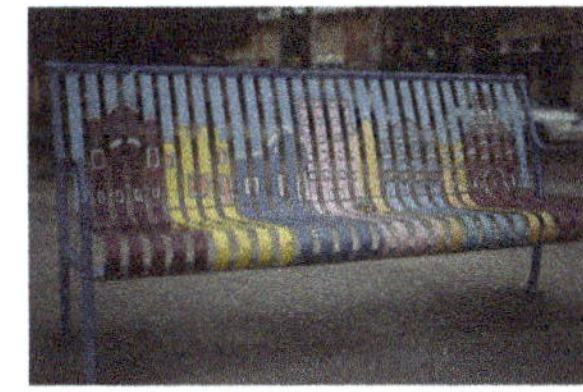

But utility boxes and benches aren't the only government structures bearing artistic expression. Downtown Lafayette's light posts and traffic light poles feature the work of local painter-sculptor Pat Juneau.

14 Diana Moore's "Urns of Justice" reflect her interpretation of her visit to South Louisiana. Read more here: http://www.gsa.gov/portal/mediaId/136682/fileName/105_Diana_Moore.action

15 This prompts some locals to comment that justice is not only blind, but at times may have no brains. Another reports that the heads were designed to be planters but a local architect objected to the plants on grounds that the sculptures would "look like Chia Pets." Proof that Lafayette natives enjoy humor in even the most serious of circumstances.

16 ArtBox, the named effort behind treating electrical transformers as canvases for local artists, is a collaborative effort between Acadiana Center for the Arts and Project Front Yard (a Lafayette Consolidated Government program) with support from the Lafayette Convention and Visitors Commission.

17 The museum is also known as The Hilliard, officially the Paul and Lulu Hilliard University Art Museum. The Hilliards chose art as part of their legacy for Lafayette.

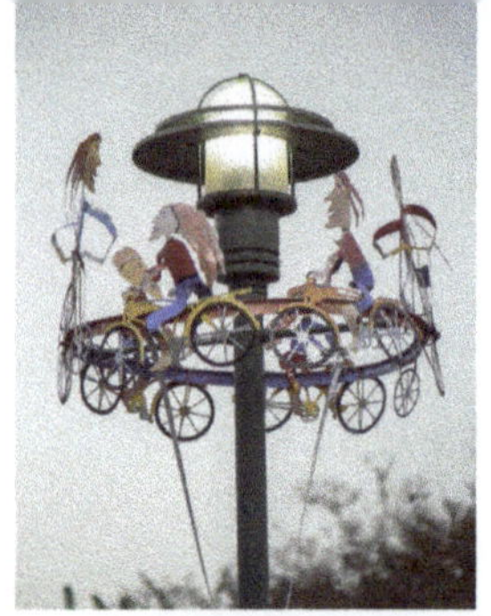

Juneau decorates what would be plain poles with flowers (one of his signature expressions) and accents the pole nearest The Lafayette Science Museum with painted sculptures of dinosaur bones.

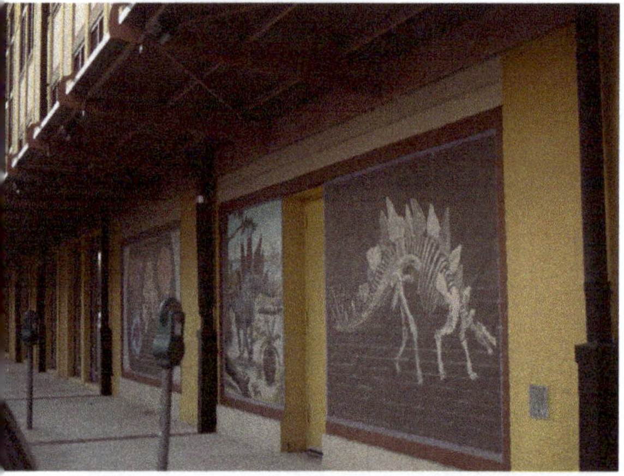

That same science museum features the work of painter Chris Pavlik who illuminated the windows along its Congress Street corridor with murals inspired by the displays within the museums walls. "I really want to use the murals to bring attention to the fascinating subjects that lie within," Pavlik told The Acadiana Advocate. His wife's pursuit of a doctorate in biology from The University of Louisiana brought him to Lafayette and he didn't hesitate to incorporate her inspiration into the works painted on the museum windows. "With my wife's science background and my mural background, it seemed perfect," Pavlik relates.

Among scientifically-inspired works stands Robert Wiggs and Rusty Bernard's DNA sculpture on Saint Mary Boulevard. Commissioned in 1987, the sculpture is a somewhat stylized but quite accurate representation of the deoxyribonucleic acid molecule we commonly refer to as DNA. The piece was intended to highlight Lafayette's commitment to modern medicine "which gives life, extends life, and improves the quality of life."[18]

The education community used art to promote art (fittingly) in its campaign known as "Pelicans on Parade." Renée Roberts explains that the idea originally began as a way for schools to promote art education awareness on campuses in the parish. According to Roberts, the then school official Burnell LeMoine saw the program as a way to create awareness for the importance of art in schools. Business leaders noticed the pelicans and requested a version for themselves. Before long private locations throughout the community featured stylized versions of the pelicans that not only supported local artists but publicly represented their desire to promote art throughout the community.[19]

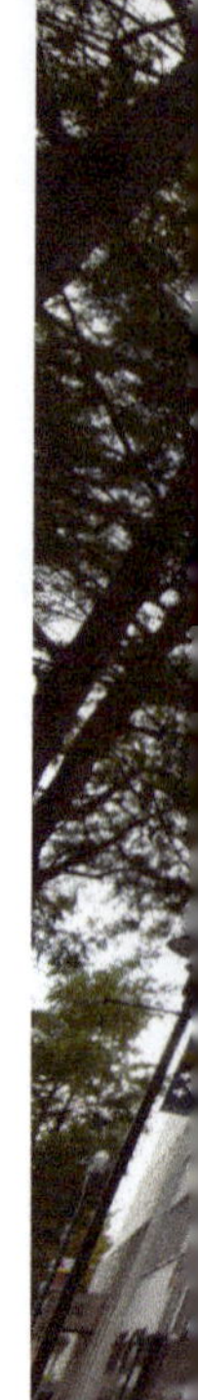

18 Quoted from a plaque still visible at the site.

19 Lafayette was among the earliest communities to adopt this form of arts promotion.

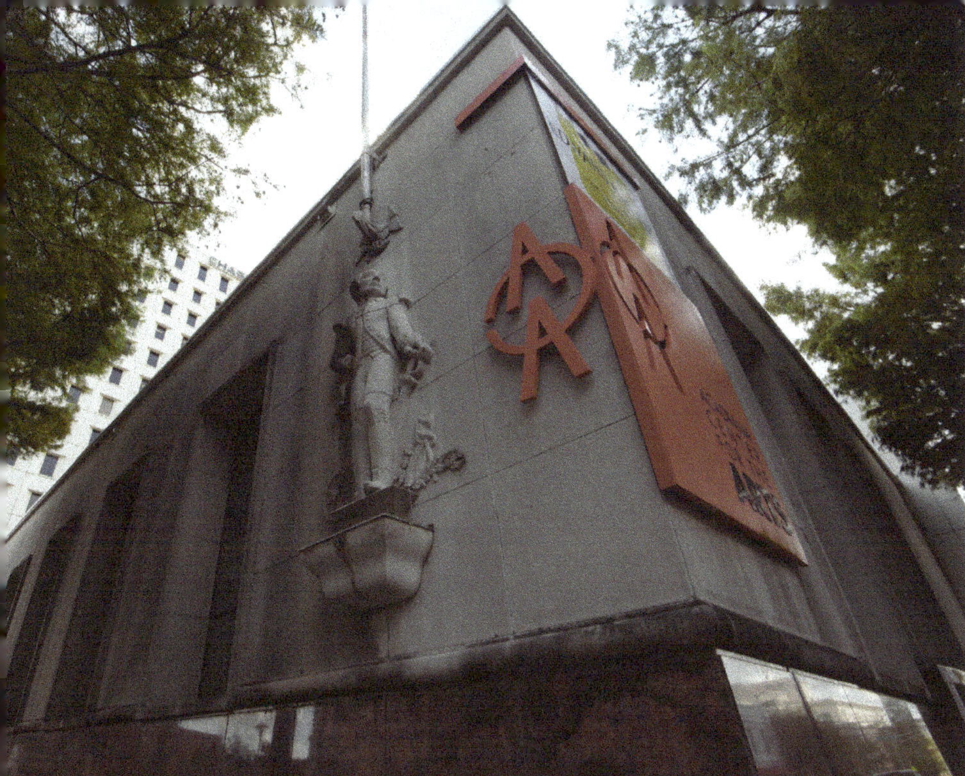

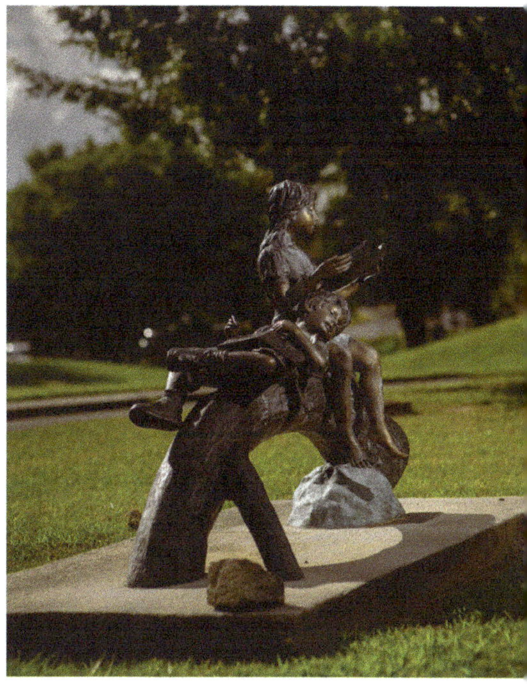

But artistic support isn't specific to education. Founders of the legendary nightclub "Scandals" saw fit to install a stained glass butterfly as a welcome piece. The sculpture now sits before the flags at the entrance to the Whyndam Garden Inn.

Bankers found it appropriate to build carved symbolic walls out of what is now Acadiana Center for the Arts (formerly LBA Bank). Rather than ordinary stone structure, they opted to feature carvings representing Louisiana's heritage. General Lafayette stands guard on the corner with Native Americans, pelicans and other Louisiana symbols flanking the Vermilion Street wall of the building.

Perhaps children read into public art more than we imagine. That may, at least, be part of the inspiration behind a bronze sculpture in front of the Child Development Center on Lewis Street. The work, created by Paul Anderson and commissioned by UL's Student Government Association, features two smiling children enjoying their time reading books. It's easy to imagine the sculpture having some influence on the young minds entering this school.

A short walk beyond the Child Development Center brings you to Fletcher Hall, home to the university's art and architecture department as well as a good spot to find public art, which is often the product of student and professor's imagination.

Of note are the large "sticks" or "poles" along Girard Park Drive. They're the creation of Architecture Professor George Loli and have graced the façade for decades.

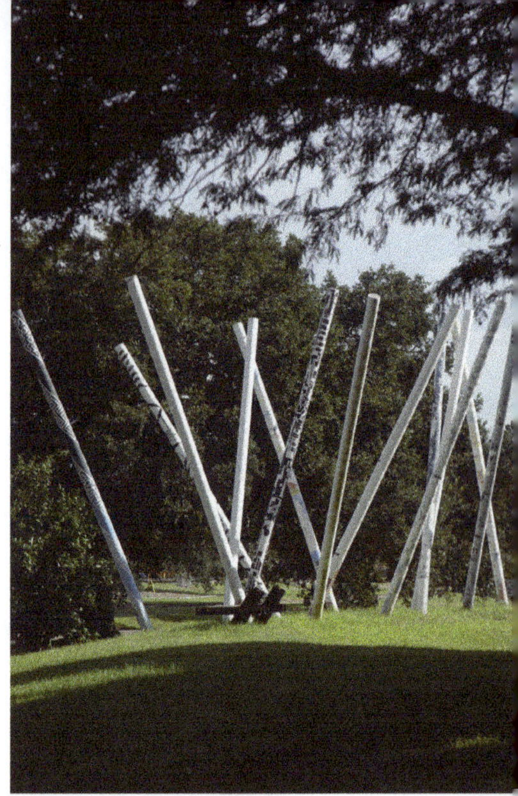

Lafayette, like many US cities, has a large number of monuments dedicated to public officials, civic heroes, military officers and deceased loved ones. The stories behind each would fill an entire book on their own — yet some deserve to be noted in this collection, as they blend the boundaries between pure monument and artistic expression. Of particular interest are the Rosa Parks sculpture, the Lafayette Firefighter and the Bendel Angel.

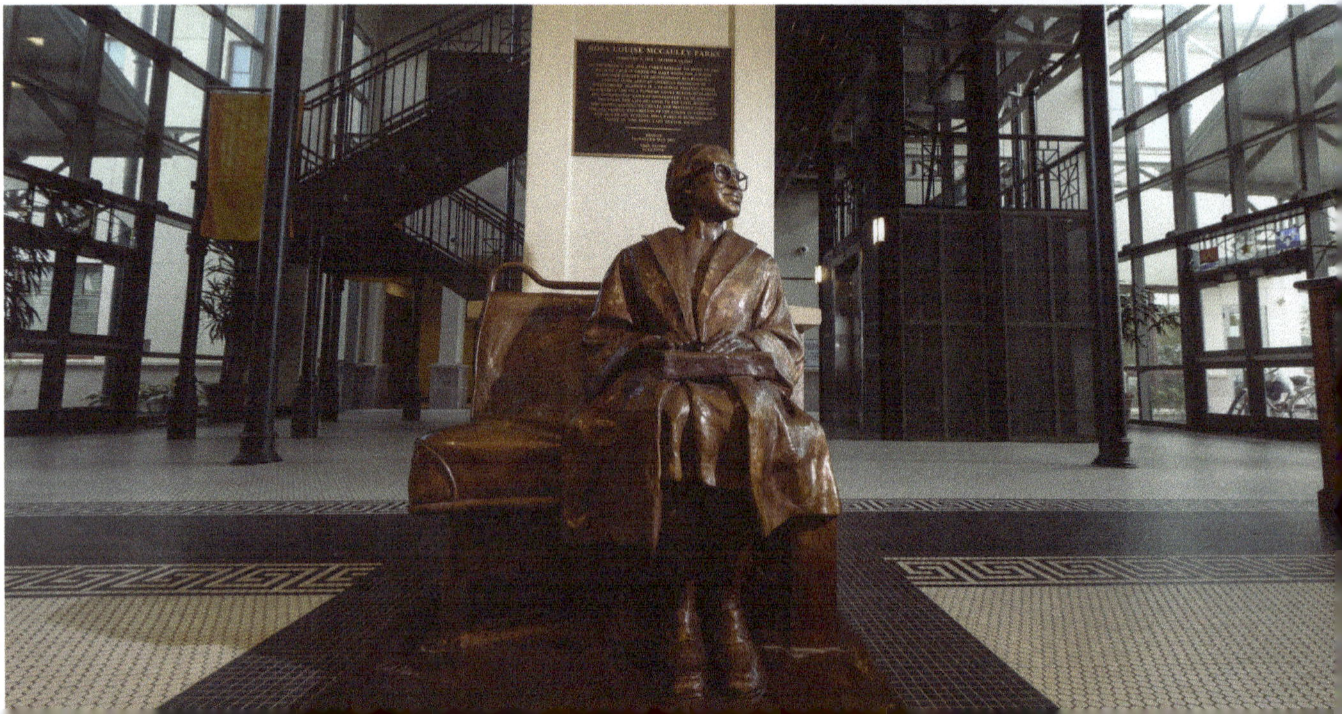

You may not be able to walk in her shoes, but you can sit next to Rosa Parks. The bronze sculpture honors Parks' brave stance against segregation and fittingly welcomes visitors to the bus station's main atrium. Artist Erik Blome built a national reputation for creating bronze sculptures that convey the emotions of historic moments. This work invites you to sit next to Rosa Parks, whether for a photograph or to imagine yourself in that moment. As described in the neighboring plaque, her seemingly individual act ignited a movement that led to the Montgomery bus boycott and, eventually, a United States Supreme Court ruling declaring Alabama's segregation laws to be unconstitutional.

Downtowners will note a prominent sculpture of Facebook fame . . . the Lafayette Firefighter. The monument was created in 1970 by Roudley LeBlanc and Nugier Perrodin (both assistant fire chiefs). The statue honors firefighters who lost their lives in the line of duty. The work's prominent location and bright white surface makes it easy to spot and popular to photograph, so much so that a fence was needed to keep the sculpture intact.

Lafayette historically welcomed and nurtured the ideas and dreams of citizens from a range of cultures. Early Jewish settlers contributed greatly to the development of the town, to such a great degree that they inspired then Governor Mouton to donate land in the city as Hebrew Rest Cemetery. Peek through the trees from Lee Street

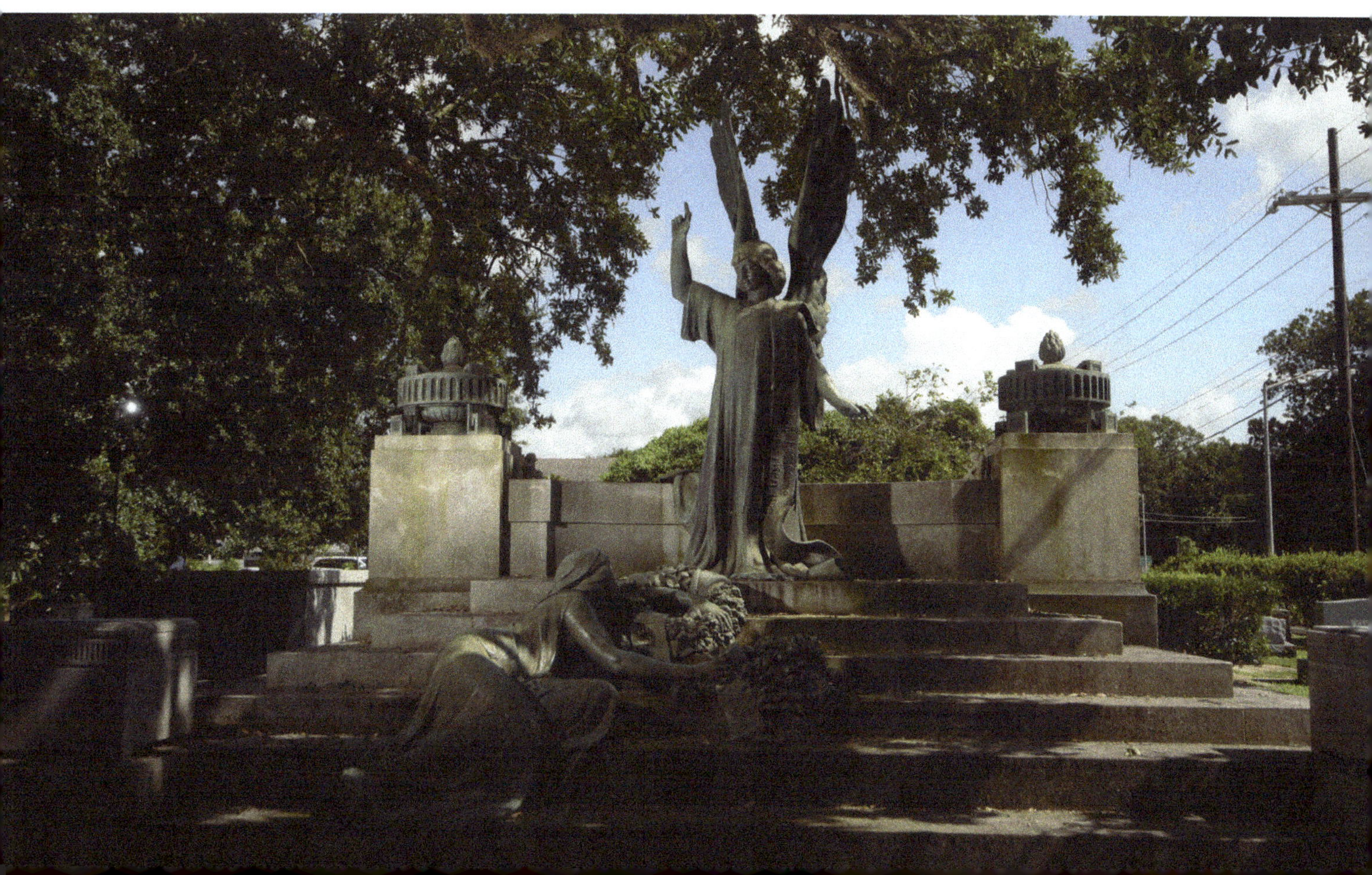

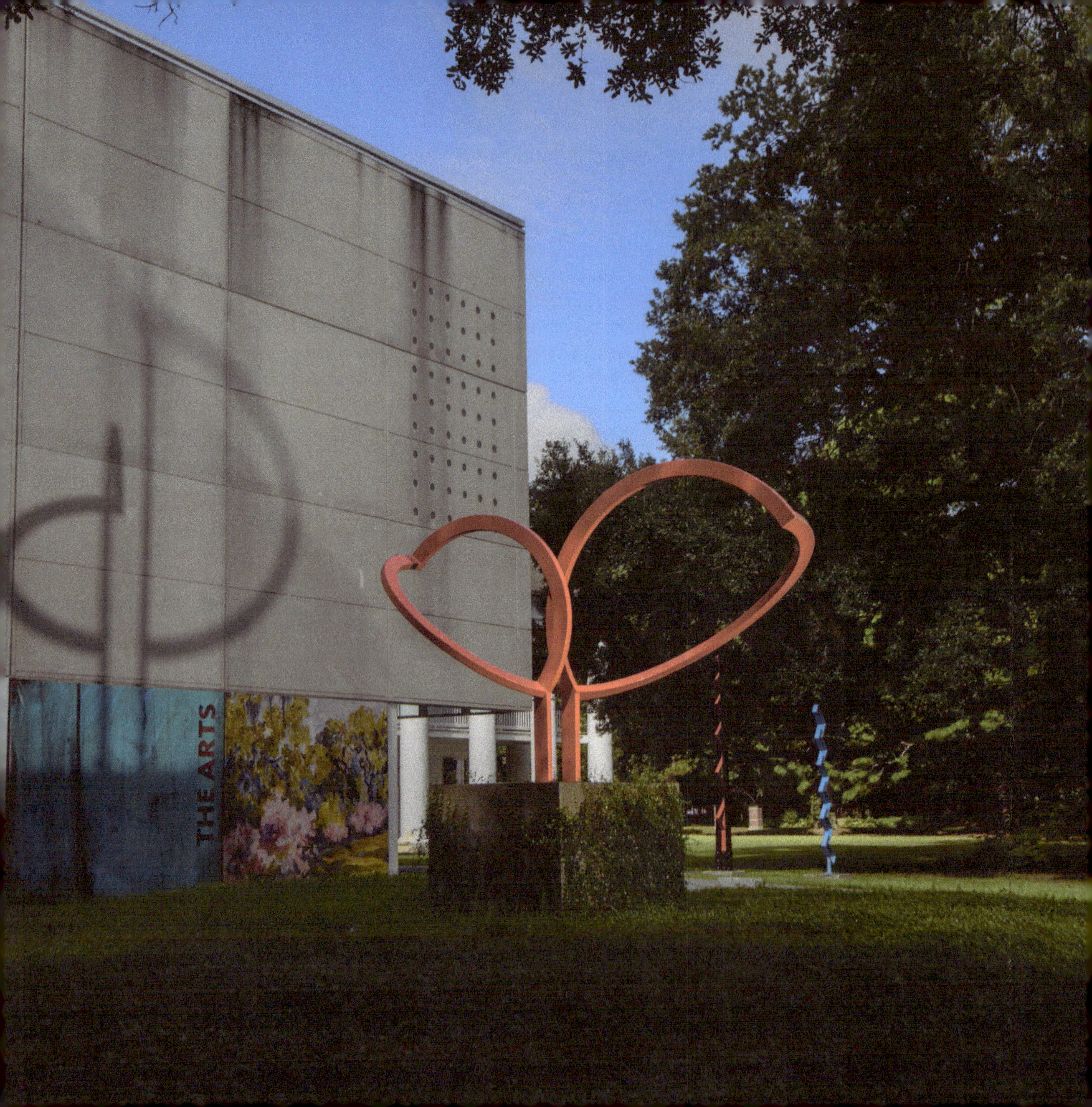
THE ARTS

and you'll get a glimpse of the Bendel[20] monument, a towering angel casting a sympathetic yet reassuring stare toward a woman who lies weeping across the steps below. The work was commissioned by famed boutique owner and designer Henri Bendel.[21] Sources say the world-renowned sculptor Charles LeMarquier rendered the piece, which was cast in Italy. Once shipped to Lafayette, it was hauled by horse and cart to the site. The weeping woman is said to be Henri and brother Isacc's mother.

Lin Emery's kinetic sculpture spins slowly before the Knight Oil Tools building on Evangeline Thruway. The work was commissioned by the company at the opening of their new headquarters. Emery chose marine aluminum, polished to a chrome-like finish and shaped into her signature circular design connected by branches. The New York native now lives in New Orleans. The fluid movements of her work are often compared to ballet.

The Hilliard, The University of Louisiana Art Museum, hosts two sculptures and a water feature on its lawn. George Newton's "Bending the Curve" appears abstract then, as perspective changes, comes together to form a heart. In the background zigzagging kinetic sculptures click and clang while in the distance, James Garland's water feature (mentioned later in this book) beckons visitors with the soft sounds of a whispering waterfall. With a light breeze, the combination of works outside of the building provide a visual and audible hint to the art that lies within.

In addition to monuments, the city is filled with murals. Some are obvious works of commercial art while others represent pure artistic expression. Some of the most profound pieces are the work of Robert Dafford,[22] many of which have been extensively covered in Photographer Philip Gould's book *The Public Art of Robert Dafford*.[23] Other murals lie hidden in places such as the downtown parking garage where its fate in faded paint looms in the darkness. Commercial murals, such as the Dwyer's Café mural depicting its founders and workers, have the funding and support to remain updated and maintained. And recently, a trove of new painters such as Chris Pavlik, Lucas Menard and Susan David have found welcome canvases on the walls of museums and warehouses.

---

20 One prominent member of the Lafayette Bendel family was Henri Bendel. He founded a boutique that bears his name on New York's 5th Avenue . . . and you can still shop there today.

21 You can still shop at Bendel's boutique on New York's 5th Avenue (and online).

22 More about Dafford and a recent work in the pages ahead.

23 This book is thorough, intriguing and highly recommended. It can be found both online and through most bookstores.

Lafayette Gone Wilde

Plato argued that art imitates life — but that it wasn't necessarily a good thing.[14] Aristotle would back off of that definition a bit, posing the concept that art mirrors life and that it is a good thing (for lack of greater interpretation)[15]. Who was right? Well, both to some degree. These concepts were meant to make us think. And they held the world's attention until the 1880s when Oscar Wilde wrote:

"Life imitates art far more than art imitates life."

— Oscar Wilde

In his essay *The Decay of Lying*, Wilde argues that it may well be true that art imitates life. Certainly life must be at least some source of inspiration for artists. But more than art mirroring life, art shows us the beauty in life. It introduces us to seeing even the most ordinary things in ways that create a sense of beauty or even shock or sadness. What was once veiled by what we call day-to-day life is not so much mirrored as it is highlighted and reinterpreted in ways that help us see it in the first place . . . then see it in a new way.

---

14 *The Republic* is full of interesting ideas, I just don't happen to agree with this one.

15 This quote is from his work called *Poetics*, the title of which might lead you to believe he's more sympathetic toward artists.

From a Wilde perspective art points out beauty we might miss and gets us to look at it differently. We then see something we may have overlooked our whole lives in a whole new way and do that most human of things: assign adjectives. **"Did you see that mural, it's beautiful,"** or **"This sculpture is just so sad yet it makes me feel proud."**

While much of the artistic expression in Lafayette will help you see things differently in even the simplest of ways,[16] there are particular installations that bring the ordinary into new light. They help us to remember a troubled past and fill that concept with pride. They bring the most common (and perhaps overlooked) shapes in nature and fill us with the wonder of what's possible. They bring out prayerful, mystic, thoughtful, humorous, sorrowful, peaceful, heartfelt emotions. These particular works mirror a time and space and perspective that shows us something new about the things in life that sometimes may be invisible. If they get you to stop for a moment to reflect on anything, they've achieved a Wilde and wondrous new way for a community to see itself.

16 After all, who ever thought an electrical box would be a canvas?

Twisted Loop

Artist: ROBERT WIGGS

In a corner-shaped park along the downtown stretch of Congress Street sits a simple unassuming white curve. The piece is one smooth and gentle loop. Its white surface has no other designs or color. But don't be deceived by its simplicity. The work, like its sculptor Robert Wiggs, hides beneath its simple exterior, a universe of complexity and meaning.

While Wiggs was teaching art at the university level he reports being surrounded by what most artists would consider a wealth of inspiration. He referenced historic art. He could meander museums full of classical and modern art. But Wiggs wanted something new and he found it in a place few artists had gone for inspiration . . . the works of Einstein and quantum theory.

As he learned about the basic building blocks of the universe, Wiggs envisioned ways to draw, paint, sculpt, carve and, ultimately, illuminate an oft-unseen world of physical connectivity. He saw the shapes in everything, says his son Calvin.

"We would walk through the woods and he would pull together various natural objects into an organized work of art. He'd take a picture of it and we'd move on."

For Wiggs, the shapes and patterns appeared everywhere. He studied how kernels connected on cobs of corn. He found repeating sutures, or connections, in armadillo shells and pinecones. He photographed the unexpectedly symmetrical appearance of cracks in a dry mud bed. It's as if once he saw the universe this way he couldn't "un-see" it. His new vision would revolutionize his art — and advance scientific theory.

He published papers explaining how natural shapes were variations on other shapes.[14] Some were a twist. Some were a loop. Others were cubes turned inside out. The world to Wiggs was an endless pattern of connected and corresponding shapes.

---

14 His wife and sons helped him write and edit his publications. You'll even find them credited for their efforts.

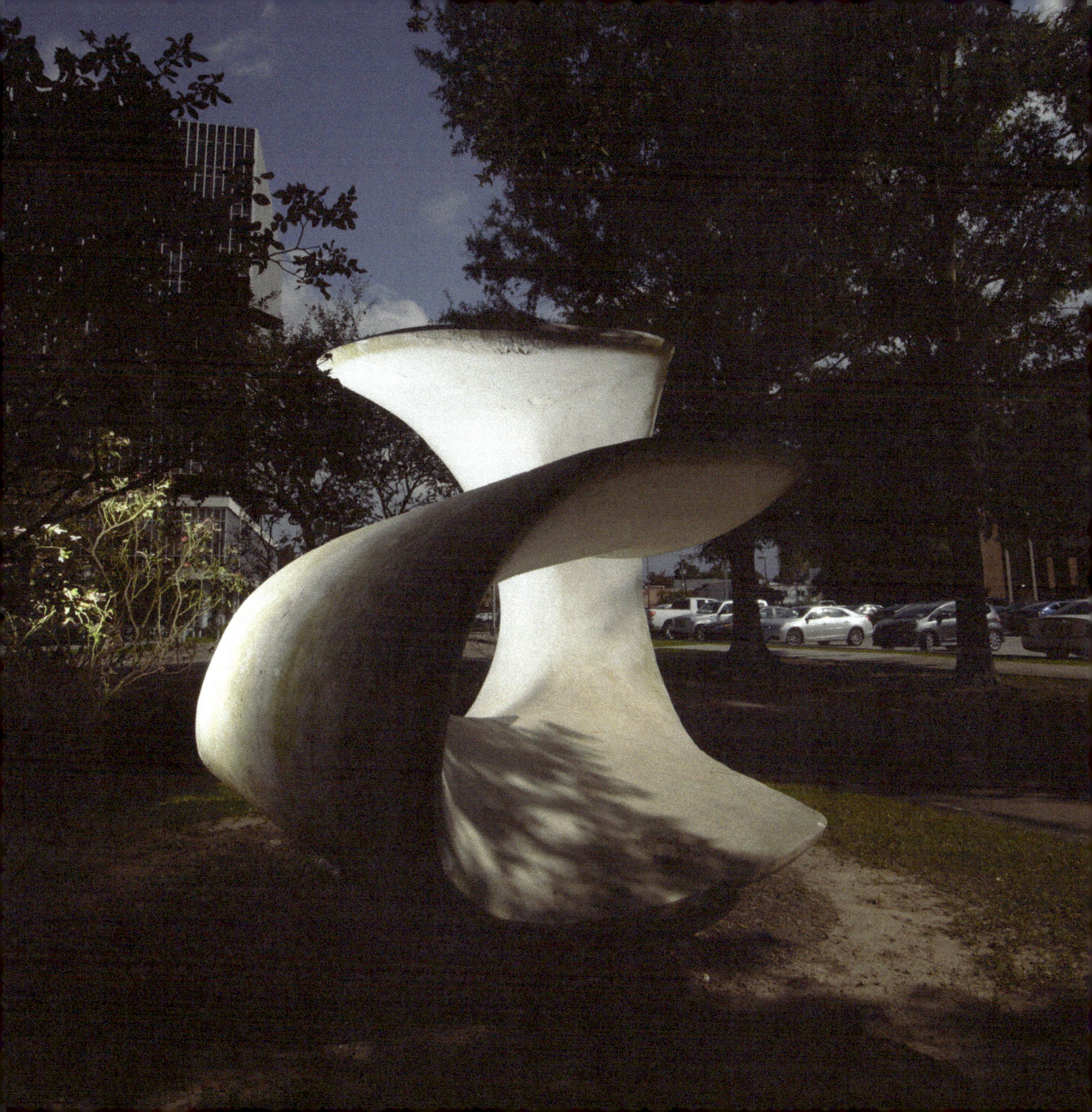

"The process of generating the forms is accomplished through a simple replication of the foundation sutures," Wiggs writes. He later differentiates his approach, "The Suture Mechanics System of generating polyhedra and lattices is different from the conventional process of constructing classical polyhedra because polyhedra are not constructed from preformed polygons but are generated from lines and their junctions."

His theoretic and artistic exploration would lead him to discover a new all-space filling form or shape, one he dubbed the "Twist Octahedron." Prior to this discovery, only eight of these forms were known. Five were discovered by ancient Greeks and the last three were discovered by Lord Kelvin, Buckminster Fuller and Keith Critchlow. Wiggs' combination of artistic vision and scientific theory placed him in the company of history's greatest scientists.

While his theories earned him respect as a scientific thinker, his art would earn the admiration of nearly everyone who saw it. Inspired by his systematic theories of shapes and connections, Wiggs would form physical versions of his theoretical shapes in wood, concrete, metal and more. Perhaps it's because humans instinctively recognize these shapes in some way, but the dramatic curves and repeating patterns of his works seem to have inspired even those who had no idea about his scientific theories. He would craft the uniquely shaped "Four Tigers" for LSU, a genetically accurate DNA sculpture along St. Mary Boulevard and the flower-like "Octaplex" sculpture in front of Jefferson Street Towers — all influenced by his original vision of shapes, sutures and a connected world.

And what about Twisted Loop?[15] It's one of Wiggs' elemental "twists" he defines in his publications. Wiggs writes, "The loop in suture mechanics is a circular ring or torus. It has no surface area and its circumferences can be infinite in scale. All of the potential twists, no matter how complex, can be performed on a single loop." An example he provides is the unending loop found around a tennis ball.

Originally the loop took center stage in the drive-through area of downtown's LBA bank.[16] When the bank was being converted to what

15 The work was referred to jokingly as "The Tongue" by Wiggs' contemporaries, including artist Ken Stansbury who helped Wiggs construct the piece.

16 In its original location it was also a "fountain" of sorts with water flowing over its long curves.

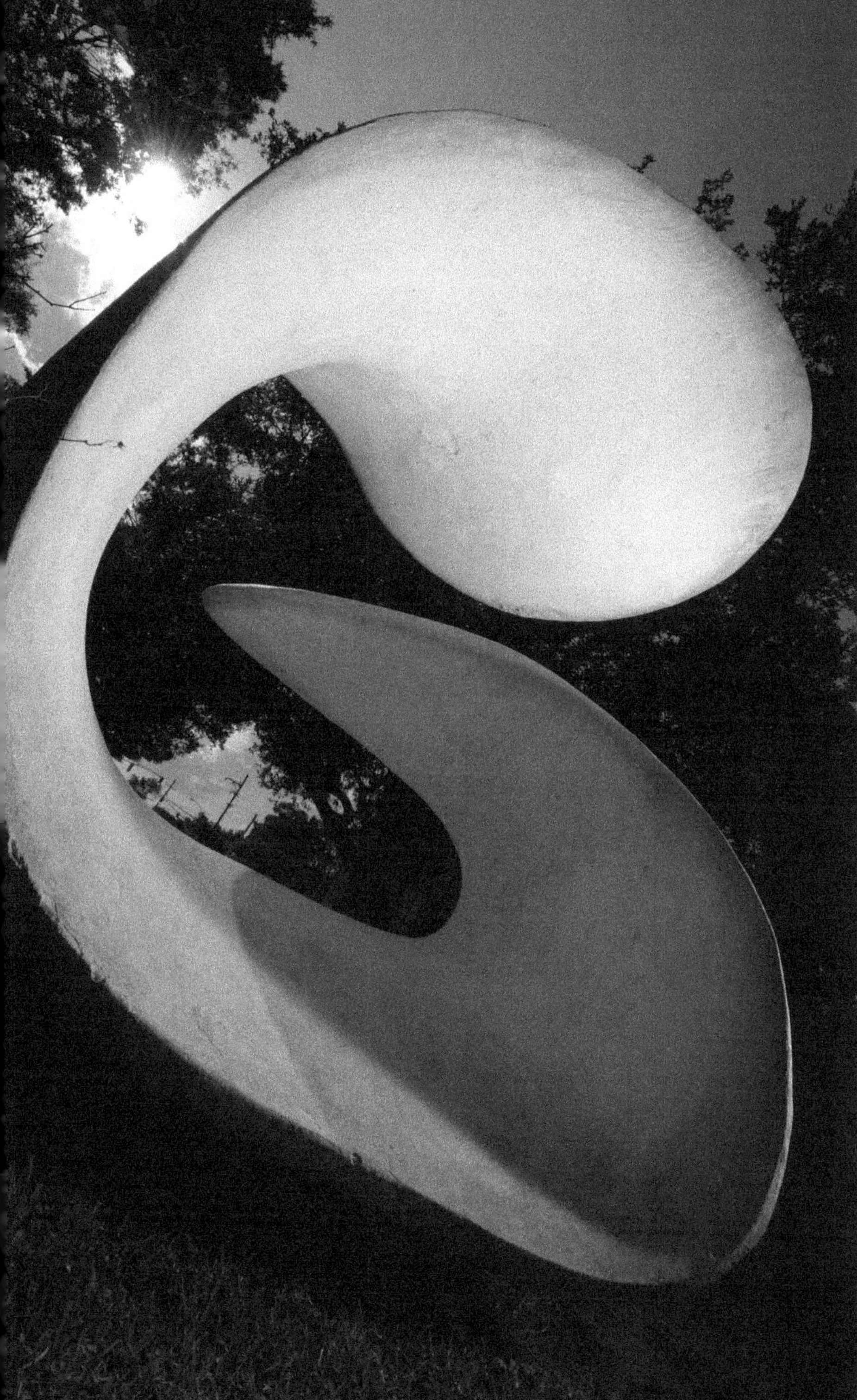

is now Acadiana Center for the Arts, there was no room in the plans for such a large structure. A collaborative effort from several organizations resulted in the loop being hoisted[17] to its current resting place.

While it may not be easy to understand the scientific significance of Twisted Loop, it's easy to appreciate its smooth, gentle form. Along the busy road way it seems to act as a road sign of its own. One that reminds us of how we're all connected . . . even in the simplest of ways.

17 The piece, made of steel and concrete, weighs in at more than eight tons.

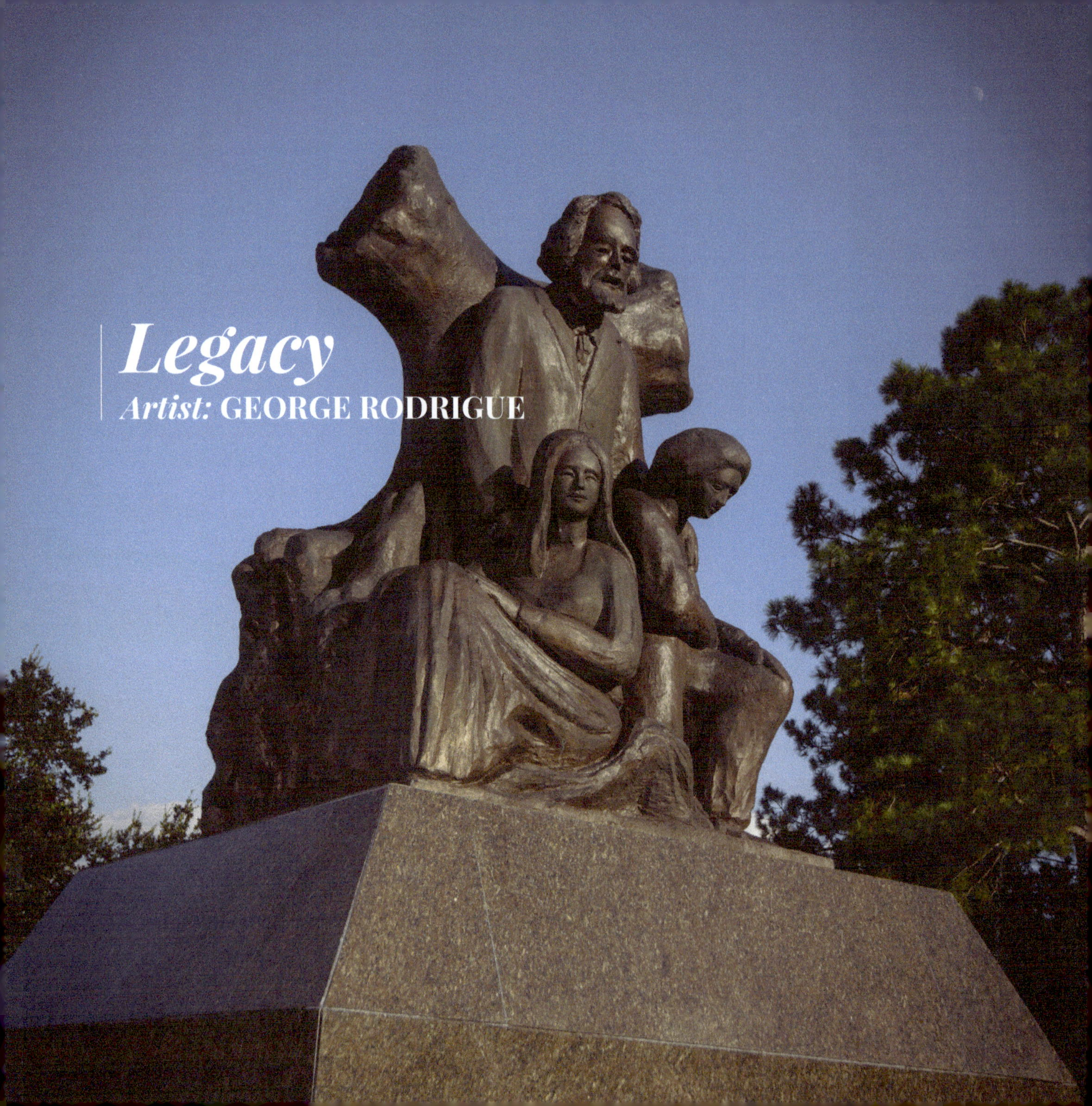

Legacy

Artist: **GEORGE RODRIGUE**

KALISTE SALOOM III BOUNCES INTO HIS SEAT AT THE TABLE BRANDISHING A SMILE THAT LOOKS AS IF HE'S ABOUT TO BURST FORTH WITH A TREASURE TROVE OF EXCITING STORIES. Because it's true. The third-generation Saloom usually goes by "Kal." It's an easier way to distinguish him from his father Kaliste Saloom Jr. — a legendary attorney and advocate of Lafayette's growth — and his grandfather Kaliste Saloom Sr. — a Lebanese immigrant who found business success in the Cajun capital.

The two elder Saloom men were involved in nearly every significant effort of Lafayette's opening history. Kal knows most of the stories about how each Kaliste helped expand the city, support the university, advocate for the arts and build successful careers as merchant and attorney. But this story — and this work of art — isn't about the Saloom men. It's about a woman and her gratitude.

Her journey begins in Lebanon. She speaks two languages: Arabic and French. Like so many Lebanese people of her era, she and her husband see the United States as an opportunity to build a successful life. Their Catholic faith and fluent French narrowed the couple's destination to the then-tiny and predominantly Cajun-French settlement of Lafayette. As she entered the country through Ellis Island, the clerk who processed her travel documents asked for her name. "Esma," she told him. Perhaps it was noisy. Maybe the clerk was rushed. For whatever reason he wrote "Asma" . . . a misspelling that would remain her moniker for life.

Once in Lafayette, the couple's idea to start a general store was welcomed and frequented by neighboring residents. As their business succeeds they invest heavily in the community and purchase farmland around the area in anticipation of developing structures that would meet the growing city's needs.

YEARS PASS.

The family grows and so does their investment success. The couple see many of their development dreams come to fruition. In the early 1980's a New Orleans investor approaches the couple with ideas for a grand office park anchored by a five-star hotel. Without knowledge of the pending oil-price crash, the couple joins the investment and the vision of Saloom Office Park begins to take shape.

Through the center of the development would lie one road that terminated in a cul de sac at the entrance of the hotel. The road would be named "Asma Boulevard"[18] in honor of the matriarch's unending support

18 Though it would always be pronounced "Esma."

for her family. At their request, a grand work of art would grace the circle. Asma seemed fairly intent about the purpose of such a work of art. It would have to be large. It would have to reflect the local style. Most importantly, explains Kal, "She wanted to honor the community . . . not Lebanon . . . not the Salooms . . . it was an homage to the culture that welcomed them so warmly."

The couple was very fond of the newly world-famous works of George Rodrigue . . . but at that time the painter had only worked on canvas. What the circle needed was a large three-dimensional work of art. The couple approached Rodrigue about the idea and it sparked his interest. As it turned out, Rodrigue felt inspired to create three-dimensional art and this would become his first commissioned opportunity.

WITH THE COUPLE'S VISION IN MIND Rodrigue went to work drafting several ideas for the centerpiece. Of the works presented, the clear favorite of both the Salooms and Rodrigue himself was a grand visual reference to Henry Wadsworth Longfellow's *Evangeline: A Tale of Acadie*. The fictional account follows its main character Evangeline as she is separated from her love Gabriel during "Le Grand Dérangement"[19] — the forceable expulsion of the Acadians from their home in Nova Scotia. Her journey ends (spoiler alert) in St. Martinville as she sits beneath a tree, patiently waiting for her love Gabriel, who never arrives.[20]

NOT ONLY WAS THIS RODRIGUE'S FIRST WORK OF SCULPTURE, IT WOULD BE HIS LARGEST.
His vision centered around a large tree (commonly referred to as "The Evangeline Oak") with cut limbs. In front of the tree is Longfellow standing with his hands on the shoulders

19 The Queen of England would eventually apologize for this: http://www.acadianmuseum.com/apology.html

20 Longfellow became famous as one of America's early mythologists, weaving facts into legend to create moving stories. Historians report that the story is believable that readers begin to believe the characters actually existed.

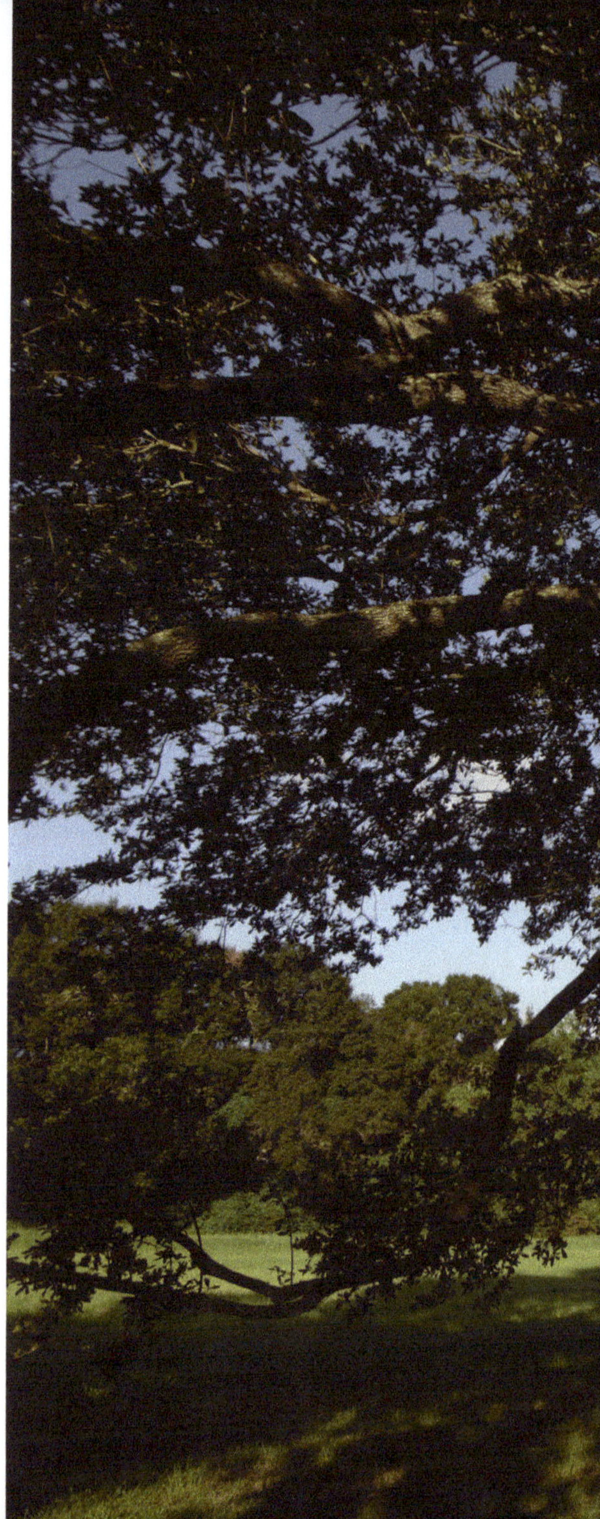

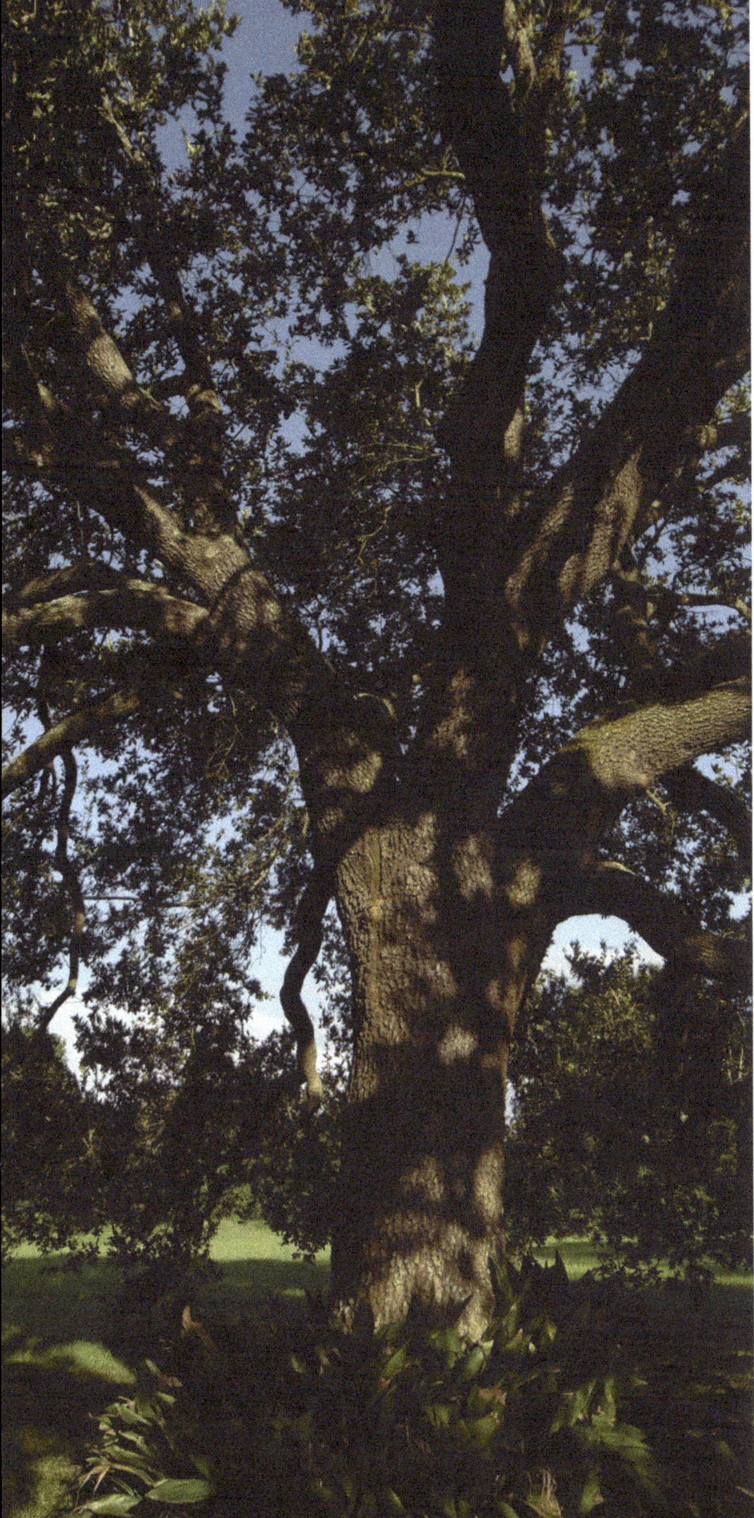

of seated Evangeline and Gabriel. The scale was so enormous no US-based foundry could cast it. Rodrigue would travel to Pietrasanta, Italy, sculpt the piece and have it shipped to its current resting place at the end of Asma Boulevard.

The work is as large as its legendary roots:. The statue stands over 10 feet in height with a seven-foot-wide base and a 28-foot perimeter. Add to that the approximately six-foot height of its marble platform and the work towers above any onlooker. Despite the sculpture's enormity, the features of Longfellow, Evangeline and Gabriel reflect the sadness of simple people swept up by forces much larger than themselves.

Wendy Rodrigue, wife of the now-deceased artist, writes in her blog[21] that her husband referenced the title as *Longfellow, Evangeline and Gabriel*. The Saloom family references the work as *Legacy*, noting the intent of their late matriarch Asma. It's easy to imagine some connection Asma may have felt with Evangeline. Both travelers from foreign lands finding new homes in Acadiana, Asma's happier life experience inspires pride in local culture and compassion for those who experienced loss along that same journey. In its presence you can't help but feel the sorrow of Longfellow's story. The sculpture embodies a sense of pride reflected by Cajuns and understood by Lebanese (and other) immigrants who found a home in Lafayette . . . and it will always connect the legacies of two women who understood each other's journey.

21 WendyRodrigue.com is filled with rich stories about her late husband's work and inspiration.

The Hilliard Museum Water Feature

Artist: JAMES GARLAND

"I believe that the most important thing in the world, visually, is sunlight," posits Artist and Architect James Garland. ***"Water is number two. And everything else, wood, glass, stone, birds, Uncle Charlie, etc. all tie for third. Water is literally, endlessly fascinating and valuable. Working with it is an extraordinary challenge and a delightful intellectual puzzle."***

The fountain whispers to you. The magnificent height of the newer glass museum and the towering columns of the former museum create the illusion of a narrowing corridor — the fountain-wall at its end seems more like a window, its slight backward lean calling you closer the way someone reclining on a couch might relaxingly offer you a seat to rest, to stay, to sip and talk. And it does talk. Water gently bubbles across the pebbled surface in fanciful patterns whispering the sweet white noise of deep sleep and ocean waves.

Garland's interpretation of time and place makes a dizzying final statement.[22] He sought to "terminate the long view with an hypnotic display, and be an object in space, and that the wall might seem like a story teller, with a visually suggested depth and regular flow action transformation, with gentle, therapeutic sounds."

22 Some inspiration for this work is rooted in New York's Paley Park fountain, considered the "first" wall of water and built in the 1960s. The designer connected the two great places, grounding the piece historically while transforming the work in a new way.

The fountain's location played an important role in Garland's design. Looking at the water feature can feel as if you're standing between two worlds. To the right, the large gallery porches of the original museum[23] remind you of classic South Louisiana estates. To the left, sheer blue-hued glass walls rise three stories high and bear a reflection of the previous museum across its sleek, modern face. In the middle . . . moving water.

23 Famed architect A. Hayes Town designed the original museum.

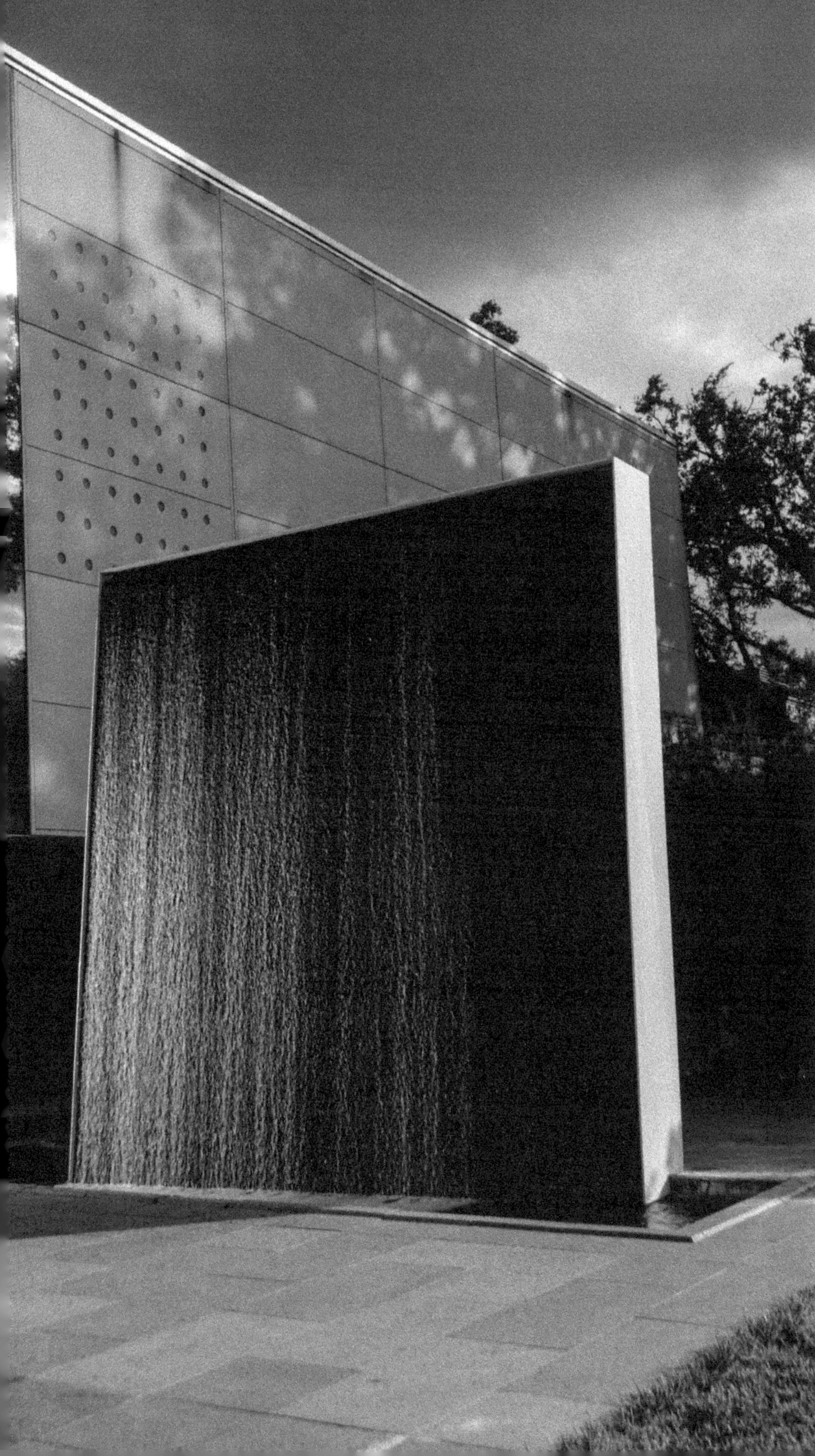

"In the built environment, collaboration is the name of the game; within that, dedication, discourse, talent and inspiration are all critical. But it's important to recognize that nothing good is accomplished without a superb client," says Garland. "This was the case for me with the [UL-Lafayette] Foundation. They were engaging, supportive, set high quality expectations, managed the money tightly and were good decision makers. For this project we developed three alternative designs. I liked them all. But the Foundation selected the correct alternative. That is to their credit."

According to The Hilliard Museum Director LouAnne Greenwald, the fountain is likely one of the most photographed locations in Lafayette. From her office she watches families, graduates, brides-to-be and more embrace the ever-changing water flow as a backdrop for some of their most important moments. On Sundays, Greenwald would peer from her office window and "a car would pull up and out would come all of this white tulle!"

Whether you're marking a milestone, biking nearby or taking in the museum's latest collection, take a moment to follow the fountain's whisper. It calls you to a space between past and future and gently reminds you that "you are here."

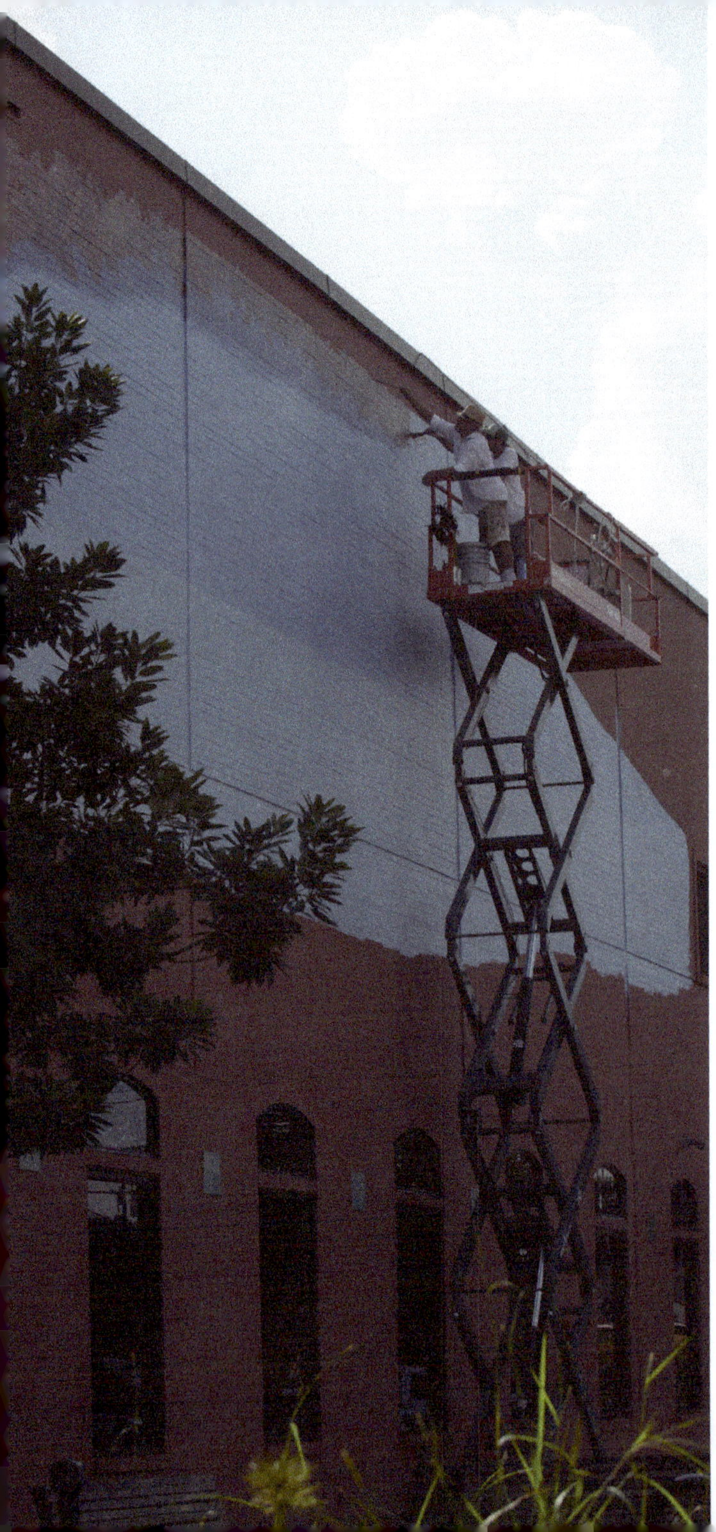

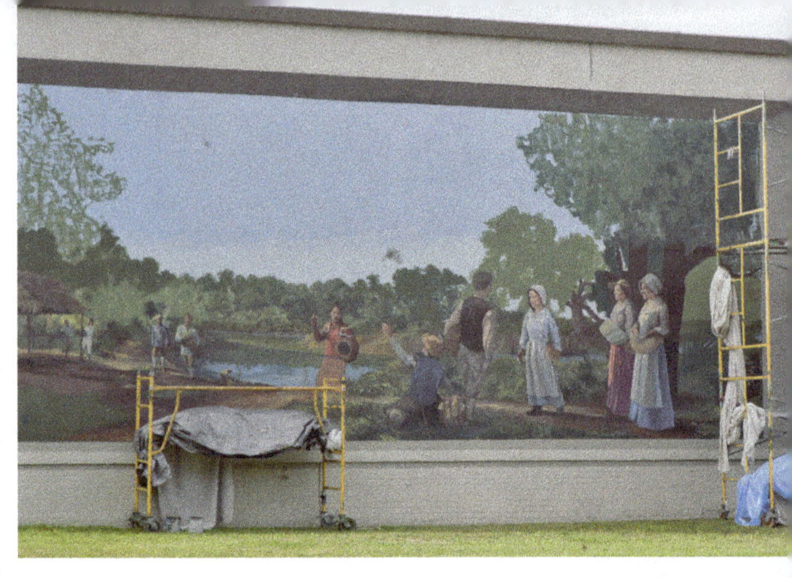

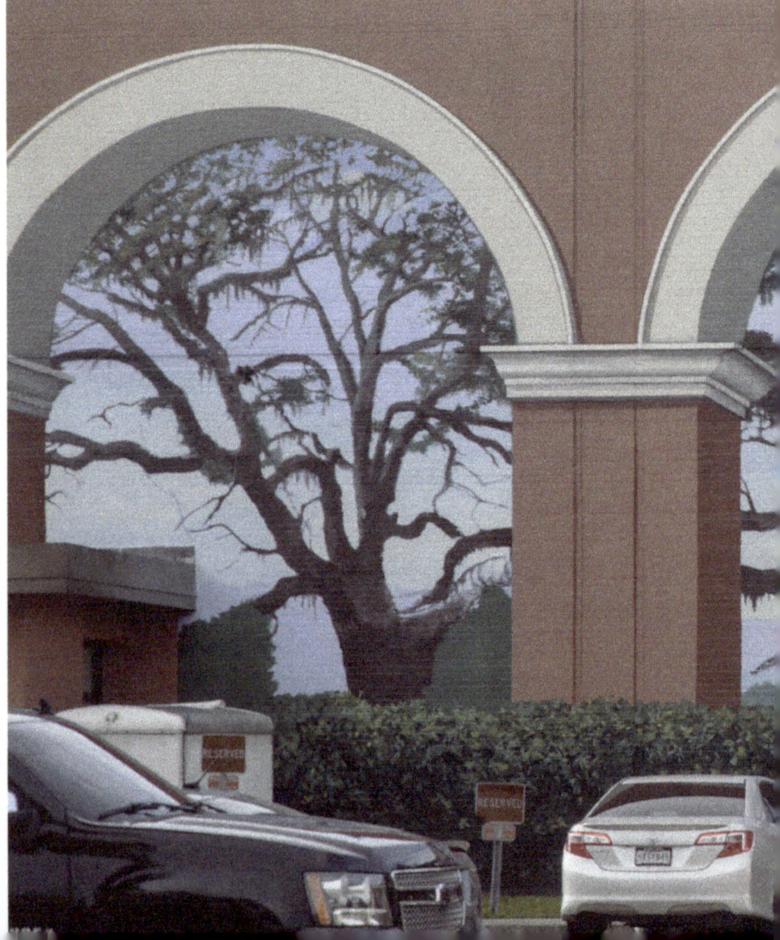

City Hall Murals

Artist: ROBERT DAFFORD

IF YOU HAVE THE GOOD FORTUNE OF MEETING DAFFORD AND HIS CREW YOU'RE IN FOR A WEALTH OF KNOWLEDGE AND SINCERE CONVERSATION. Their paint-dappled clothing makes it obvious that they're hard at work. Their warm smiles and jovial mood tells you that, to them, none of it feels like work.

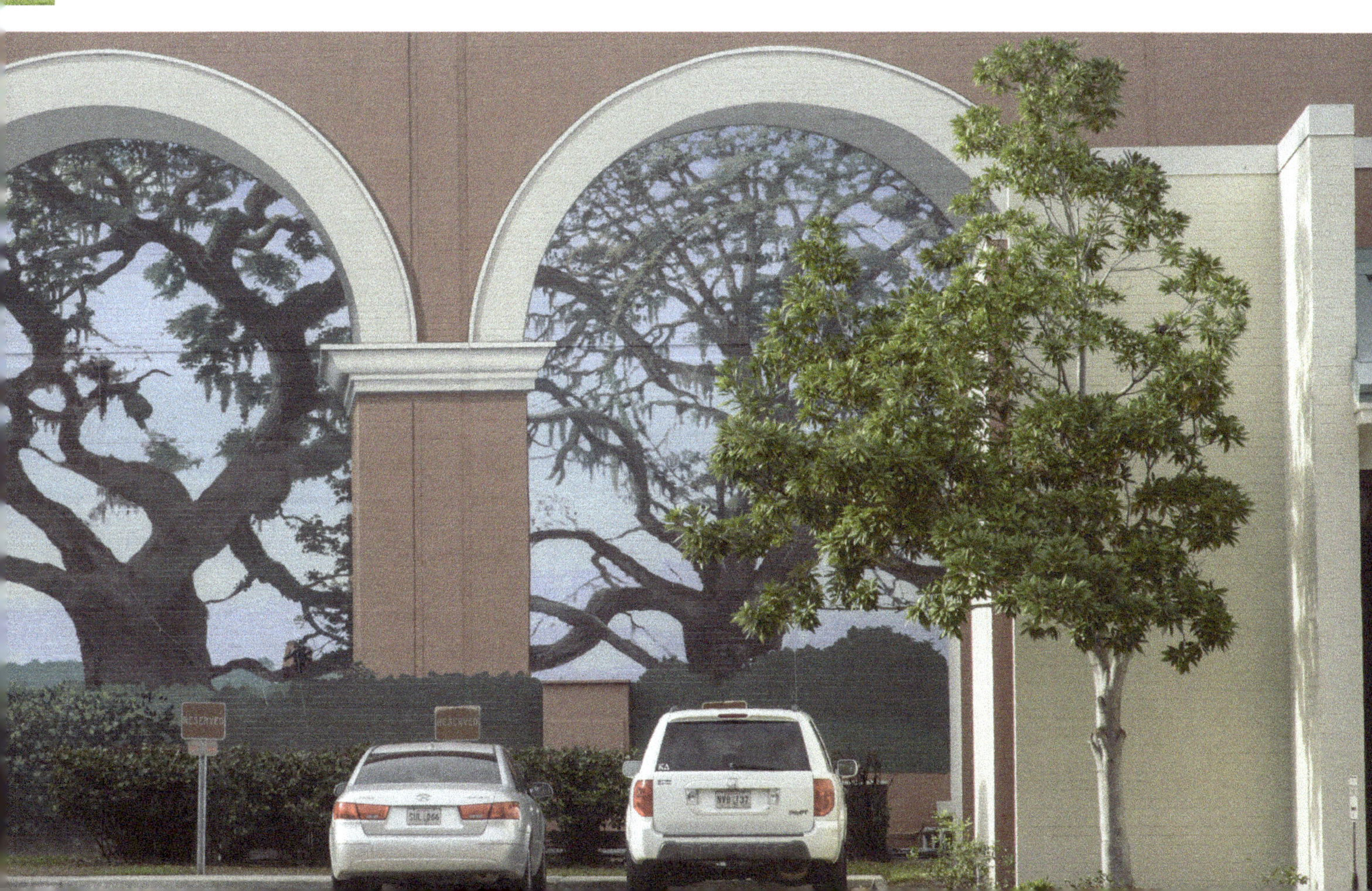

ON THE SCENE OF HIS LATEST MURALS IT'S NO DIFFERENT. Dafford carries on polite conversation as easily as his brush defines a leaf or paints a smile. The human characters in his paintings are often based on real people. He's likely photographed them in poses that reflect his vision for the mural. He references the faces for accuracy with a nearby iPad propped up by paint cans. The whole process is one, long, relaxing conversation.

Not surprisingly, that's what you'll experience from his larger-than-life paintings. In each one there is a story. In each story there are sub-stories . . . and tangents . . .

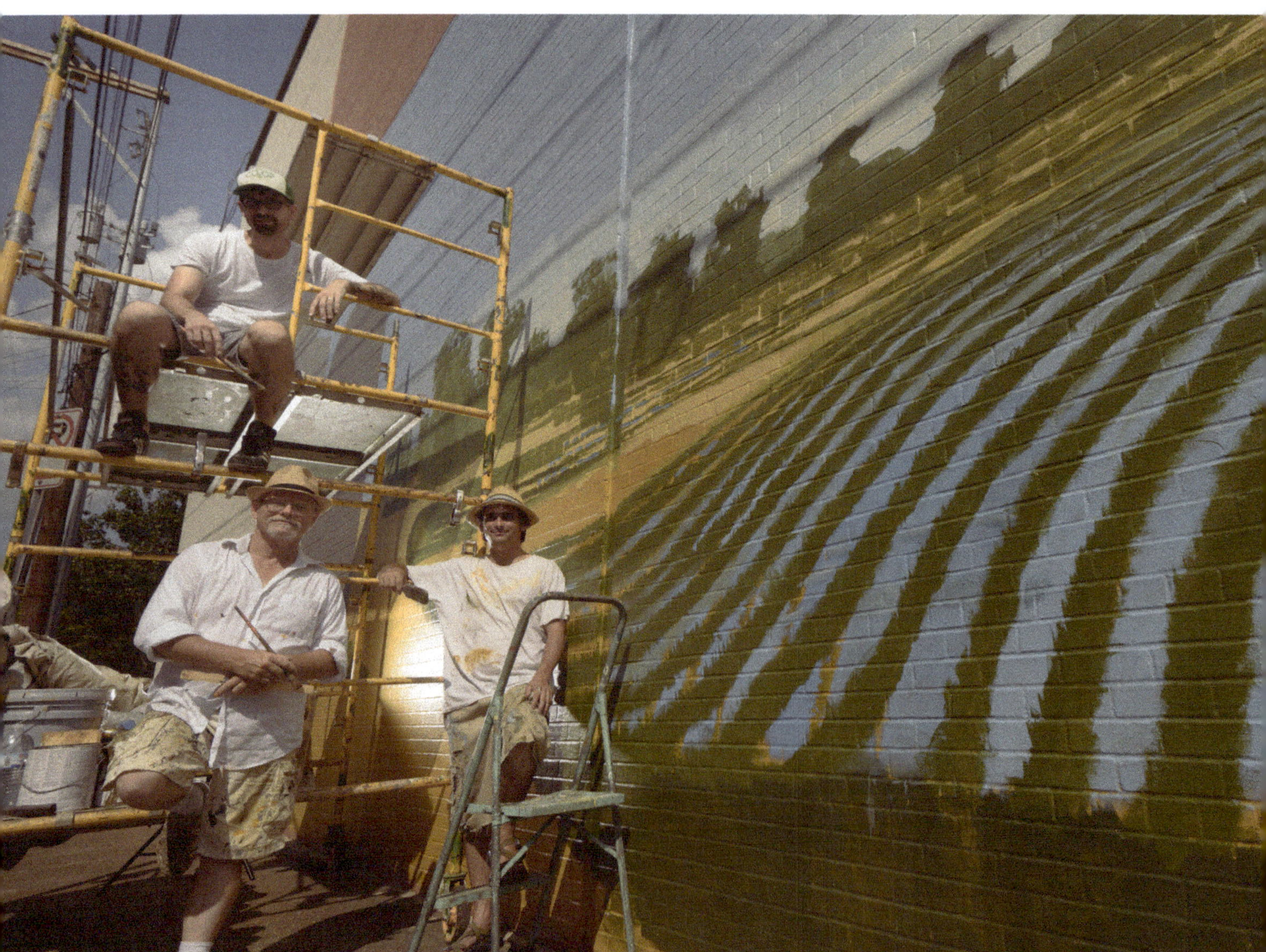

and new ideas. Looking at his work is like having coffee with a favorite friend. There's so much to talk about and you never know where the conversation will lead.

Consider that his latest installation consists of five separate murals and you'll understand that there's plenty to be said about each. On the primary façades of Lafayette City Hall, Dafford paints some of his greatest new stories:

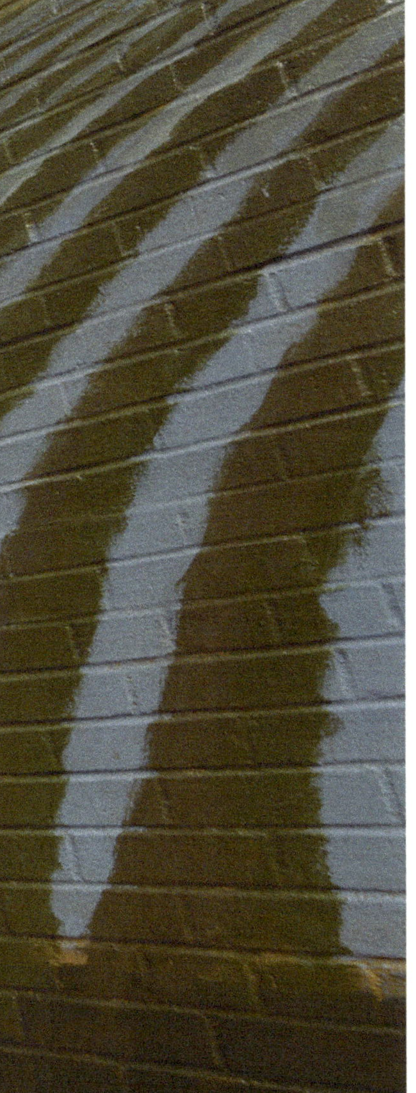

- An alcove features three massive oaks in archways. The images pay respect to the three large live oaks that were removed to build city hall.[24]
- The southern wall faces Pinhook Bridge and an area once known as Vermilionville. Hundreds of years ago, it was the gathering place for Cajun, Spanish and Native Americans to trade goods and livestock. The scene depicts what you might have witnessed back then along one of the riverbanks.
- The western wall mural turns city hall into a hotel complete with "awnings" whose painted shadows fall perfectly angled to the afternoon sun. The hotel represents Lafayette's rapid growth as the city grew westward.
- The north wall mural stretches over 200 feet in width and features a culturally iconic panorama. Fields of rice slowly transition into fields of cattle then sugar cane, representations of the area's primary agricultural commodities. Floating in the sky above the fields are staple items and images of Lafayette: Bell pepper, onion, shrimp, crab, guitar, washboard, fiddle, okra, pecan and more. There is even an image of St. John's Cathedral[25] and a roseate spoonbill.
- With the eastern wall facing Lake Martin, Dafford chose to paint an image representative of the lake's natural beauty: Cypress trees reflected in the water, the entire image framed in leaves and enveloped in a ripple effect.

With more than 400 murals in over 25 cities, Dafford is likely the most prolific muralist of our time. His works are rarely short of grand in scale and often rich with meaning and symbolism. Lafayette's city hall murals are a quintessential example of his masterful work and likely the source of many rich conversations.

---

24 One of these oaks became an artistic centerpiece in the city hall atrium.

25 The base color of city hall was chosen by Dafford to reflect the color of St. John's Cathedral just a few blocks away.

St. Philomena

Artist: SUSAN DAVID

LAFAYETTE'S JEFFERSON STREET CORRIDOR BENDS THROUGH DOWNTOWN SHOPS, RESTAURANTS, GALLERIES, OFFICES AND BARS. THE STREET IS DRESSED COLORFULLY YEAR-ROUND. Light posts are adorned with cut-metal scupture.[26] Vibrantly painted park benches display the work of a variety of artists. Robert Dafford's murals tower above the street telling symbolic stories of cars and the Atchafalaya Basin. Crosswalks and signs about art are made of graffiti hearts and spray-painted arrows. The street's concentration of creative expression hints to you that it's a regular venue for festivals, concerts, art shows and more. It boldly states that this is a place people play ... and what better décor than the expression of local artists?

Tucked within an unnamed alley behind Jefferson lies one of downtown Lafayette's newer works executed in a newer, local style. In April of 2016, while somewhat concealed in this less-traveled alley, Susan David absorbed the echoes of live music from Festival International[27] and, on the back-alley wall of a skateboard shop, painted two images of a saint.

Saint Philomena, to be precise.

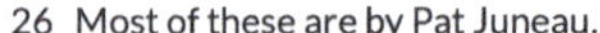

26 Most of these are by Pat Juneau.

27 Festival, as locals know it, is the largest Francophone concert festival of its kind. Oh, and it's free. More info at FestivalInternational.org.

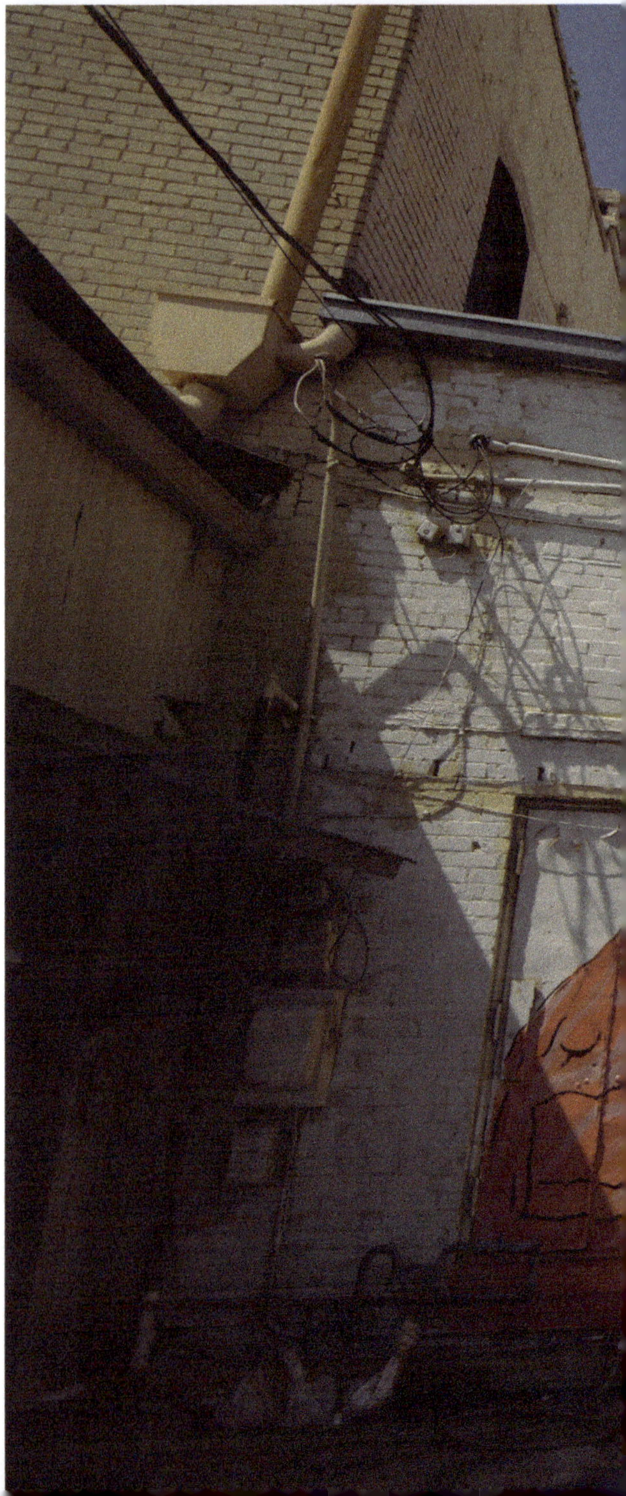

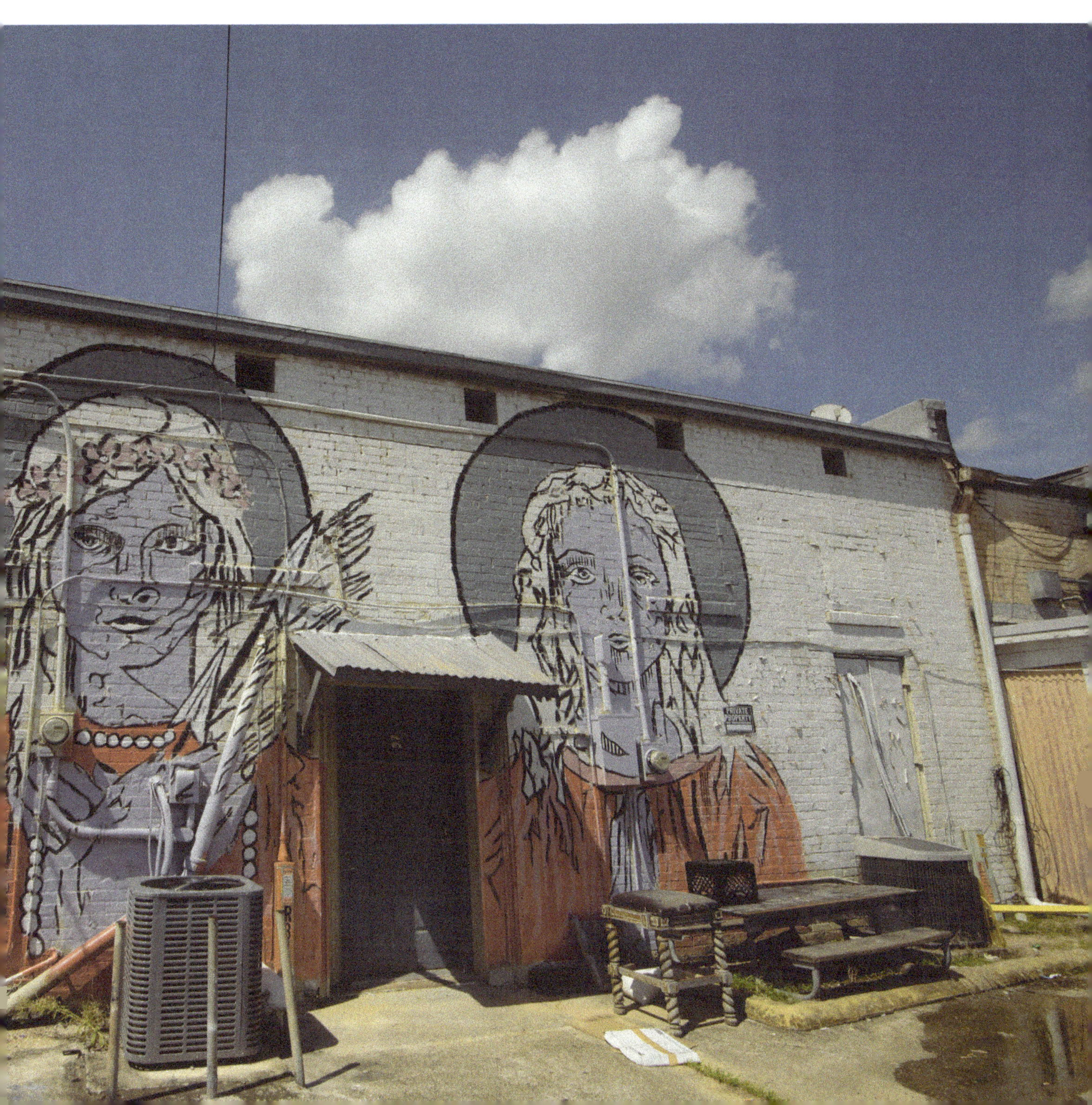

On the left, the saint is depicted with a palm and arrows, the palm representing her martyrdom and the arrows symbolizing her torture before death. On the right, she is depicted in prayer.

According to several references, Philomena, a 13-year-old of noble Greek birth, refused the Roman Emperor's request to marry. The Emperor didn't take the news lightly and had Philomena tortured in the hopes she would change her mind. She didn't. When torture didn't works she was executed. Today the saint is revered by countless followers and remembered often in prayer and adulation.

SO WHY IS SAINT PHILOMENA ON THE BACK OF A SKATE SHOP?

"She's the patron saint of lost causes," David replies. A perfect match for the rebellious nature of skate board themes.

David adds that it's entirely appropriate to have an image of a saint in this traditionally Catholic area of the world. When she looked at the wall she knew the saintly image was somehow appropriate. It was when she connected that initial vision with the story of Philomena that the work seemed certain.

The twin images stare at you with two separate expressions. The arrow-palm-holding image conveys a serious, knowing sensation. Her dress is more elaborate and the added crown of leaves alludes to her royal birth. The image on the right, though painted similarly, conveys an entirely different sense of emotion. She is humbly dressed and veiled, no crown. Her hands are in prayer and her eyes are ... sad.

THE MURAL IS WORTH EXPERIENCING IN PERSON.

You'll find it more easily by first locating one of Lafayette's iconic diners Dwyer's Café, on the corner of Jefferson and Garfield Streets. Behind Dwyer's (along Garfield) is the entrance to the alley and the painting is a short walk away.

David has no plans to stop painting murals anytime soon.[28] She painted an enormous octopus on a warehouse at the corner of Refinery and Stewart Street and is completing a giant squid on the back of the Garfield Street warehouses next to the venue Warehouse 535.[29] In addition to cephalopods, her very public portfolio includes the Two Faces of Janus, a painted elaboration of the Roman god Janus' ability to know both the past and the future.

28 David's nonprofit "Roosters Teeth" organization allows community service workers to log hours by helping to paint her enormous murals.

29 Try not to startle Susan if you find her painting in town. She won't hear you as she usually works with ear buds blaring the sounds of Radio Soul Axe or David Bowie.

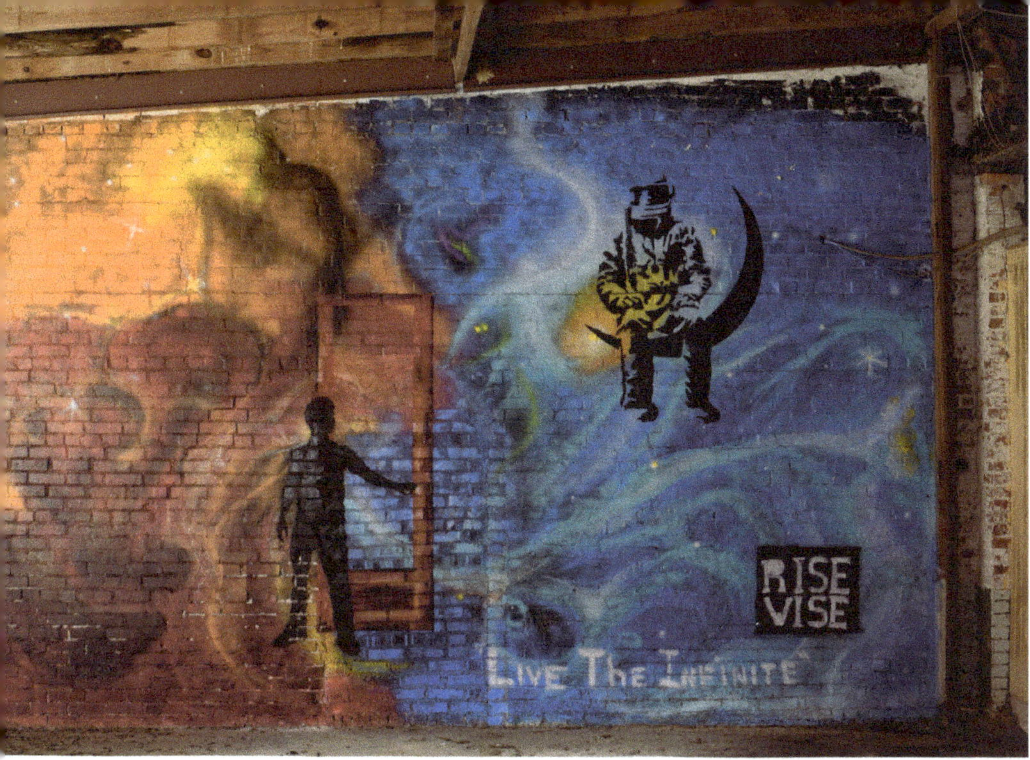

Live the Infinite

Artist: JUDE LEONARD

Tucked within a former loading bay in the heart of downtown, a spaceman and a little boy beckon you to reconsider your potential as something less finite and concrete than you might imagine. On the brick wall images of space, stars, nebulae and the moon build a dreamy idea that marked a very clear moment for artist Jude Leonard.

"My painting started with that piece," explains Leonard. "It's just exploded since then."

Now an Austinite, Leonard could never forget his Louisiana roots. "I was born in New Orleans and when the tech boom was just blossoming my family move to the Bay Area of California," he remembers. "I was always drawn back to Louisiana so I worked as a commercial diver in the Gulf of Mexico and lived in Lake Charles. That's when I decided to go to school in Lafayette."

With friends and family supporting him, Leonard pursued a degree and played music in his off hours. He formed a small band, dropped in on open-mic nights and entertained patrons at formal and informal venues. "The music thing is there," Leonard expresses. "Music is huge in Lafayette. Zydeco. Blues. Country. Whatever."

But music wasn't Leonard's only dream. He imagined himself as a visual artist and his first work, "Live the Infinite", tells the story of his leap into that world.

"What it meant to me is that it's opening the door into a giant nebula and he's taking that leap, that proverbial leap, overcoming a fear that's holding all of us back," elaborates Leonard. "So that boy is living the infinite possibility of what

:hat dream can fulfill and] he's greeted by :he Man on the Moon, :his iconic goal."

_eonard's iconic goal :ame to life with that piece. Now actively engaged in a visual arts career, he harbors ond memories of his former Lafayette home. think Lafayette s an incredible art community," he recalls. "Visual art is blossoming. I think there's room to grow and I think there's a lot of opportunity for that growth."

Experiencing *Live he Infinite* can be its own challenge, but a worthwhile endeavor. From the corner of Vermilion and Buchanan streets head south on Buchanan and take an immediate right into the first alley. You'll find the work of art just a few buildings n on the right.

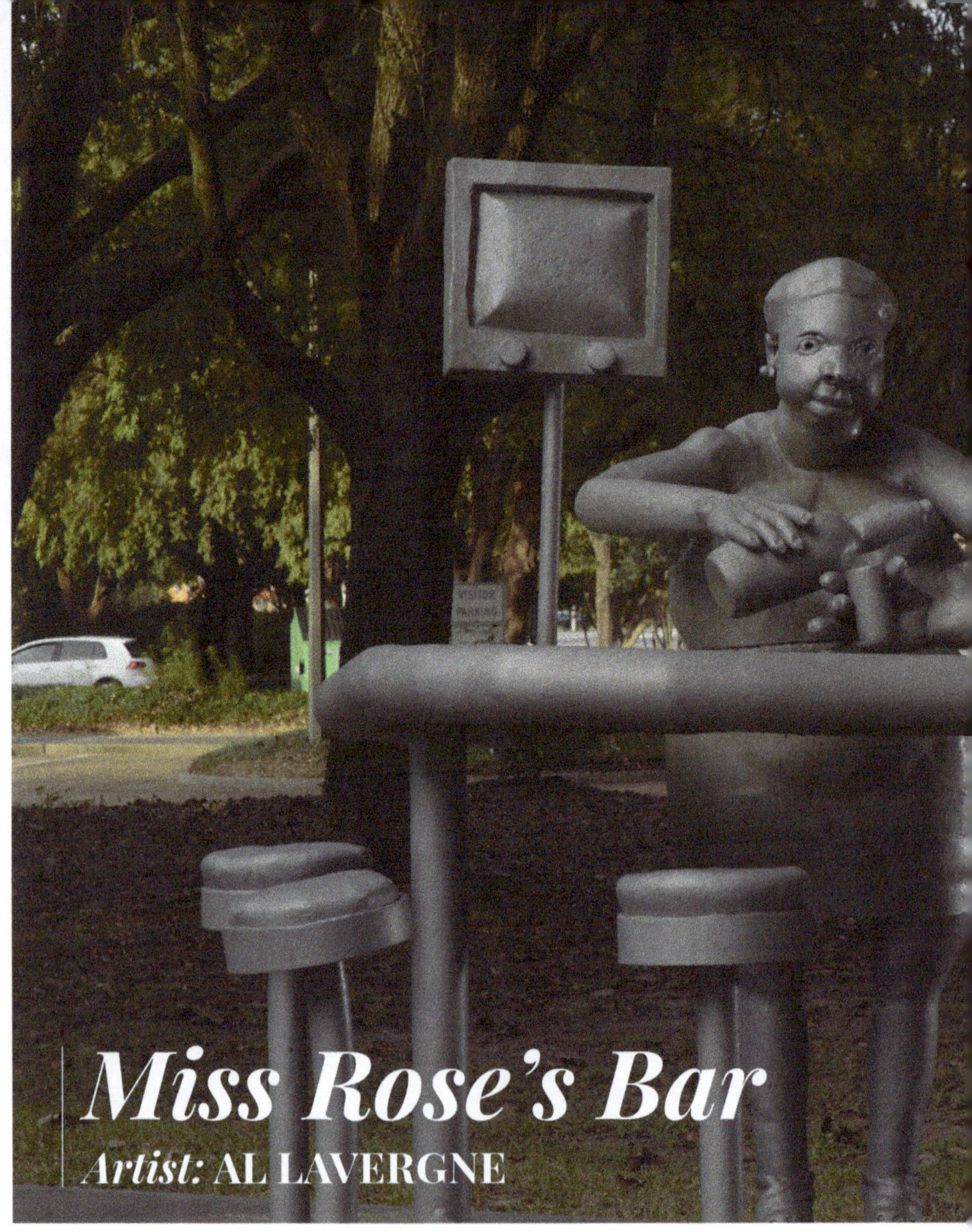

Miss Rose's Bar

Artist: AL LAVERGNE

FEW SCULPTURES CAPTURE LAFAYETTE'S CULTURAL RICHNESS THROUGH HUMOR AND FUN LIKE *MISS ROSE'S BAR*. The work brings a smile to visitors and locals comment about how it reminds them of iconic hangouts such as City Bar in Maurice, Café des Amis in Breaux Bridge or Fred's in Mamou. Though many

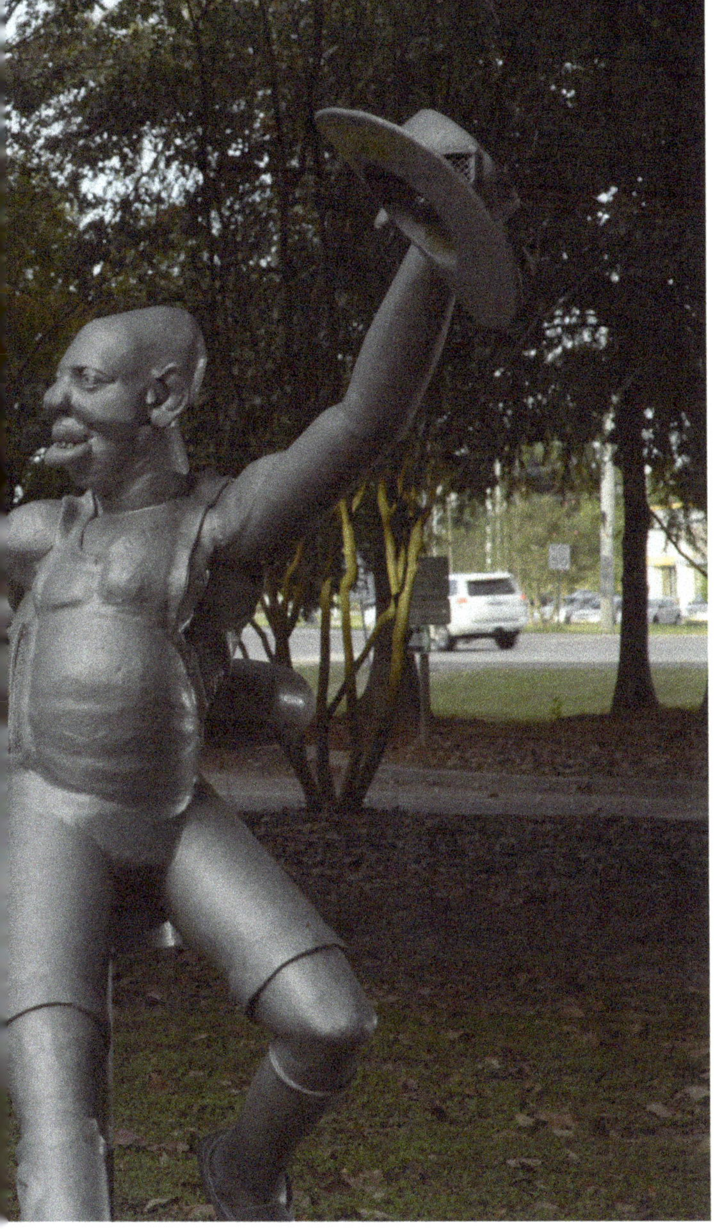

locals can feel a connection to the work through past experiences of fun and drink, its inspiration has roots in the pre-civil-rights era that often suppressed such merriment for African Americans in the South.

"In the communities of the 1950's and 60's, many black citizens were not welcomed at country clubs, recreation centers or city halls," LaVergne writes. "When there was a need to socialize or discuss current events, often the neighborhood bars, barbershops and churches were the only venues available to serve these interactions."

The sculpture highlights the importance of these venues as well as the importance of valuable time spent together, something the artist refers to as the glue of a community. "The sculpture is dedicated to the humanitarian contributions these bars made to America's prosperity," said LaVergne.

Born to a sharecropper in Basile, Louisiana, LaVergne's early experiences shaped much of his art. The artist writes about building clay models with his brothers on his childhood farm. He discusses the creativity of quilt making and experiences watching the local blacksmith build and sharpen tools. Today those influences are present in the intricate sculptures of hands and faces, in the fun-loving works of people dancing and in the tense and passionate symbols of social change.

"Miss Rose's Bar" was originally created for the 1984 World's Fair in New Orleans. Following the fair its fate was uncertain. It wasn't until 2002 that it was found in a field near Basile, rusted and worn. Volunteers from Lafayette restored the work to its original brilliance. Today you can find the sculpture in a fitting home for fun-loving viewers — greeting visitors at the Lafayette Convention and Visitors Commission information center on Evangeline Thruway.

The Dr. Seuss Wall

Artist: LUCAS MENARD

BY THE TIME YOU READ THIS STORY THE WORK BEING DESCRIBED WILL LIKELY HAVE FADED AWAY. That's because *The Dr. Seuss Wall* is drawn in chalk. It's intricate, emotive, timely, informative . . . and temporary.

The thought of putting hours, perhaps days of effort into creating something that would last a short period of time is reminiscent of Tibetan Buddhist sand mandalas. The art's temporary nature changes its purpose. It becomes a process of transformation regardless of outcome.

"I do often get asked why [I do] such large time-consuming work that will just be washed away," Menard says. "I just want to make something fun that people enjoy looking at. It's no different than someone spending so much time creating a beautiful garden. Flowers die and at some point all your hard work will be gone. That isn't a reason not to do it in the first place."[30]

The Dr. Seuss Wall was an opportunity born from another opportunity, Menard explains. When he noticed an empty wall at Lafayette's Science Museum he saw a chance to create a large-scale portrait. The museum agreed and soon the artist was able to draw the image of Neil DeGrasse Tyson, legendary scientist, science advocate and host of NOVA.

Menard's work at The Science Museum put him in position (literally) to notice the empty wall on the neighboring Children's Museum. Inspired by his success with the Tyson image he felt confident that he could create an even larger image . . . this time of the iconic children's book author Dr. Seuss.

Many people would recognize the characters in Dr. Seuss' books if Menard had drawn them across the museum wall, but the lack of recognition speaks to the life and mission of the museum. It's as if the act of asking (and finding out) about the portrait becomes part of its purpose. It reminds us that so many people who dedicate their lives to helping children are quietly unrecognizable.

30 We're glad to give the Dr. Seuss Wall more permanence by including it in this book. By the time you read this the artwork may be gone. But since the process may be just as important as the result, visit this link to see a time-lapse video of the portrait as it comes to life: https://youtu.be/u62qqWB0hGI

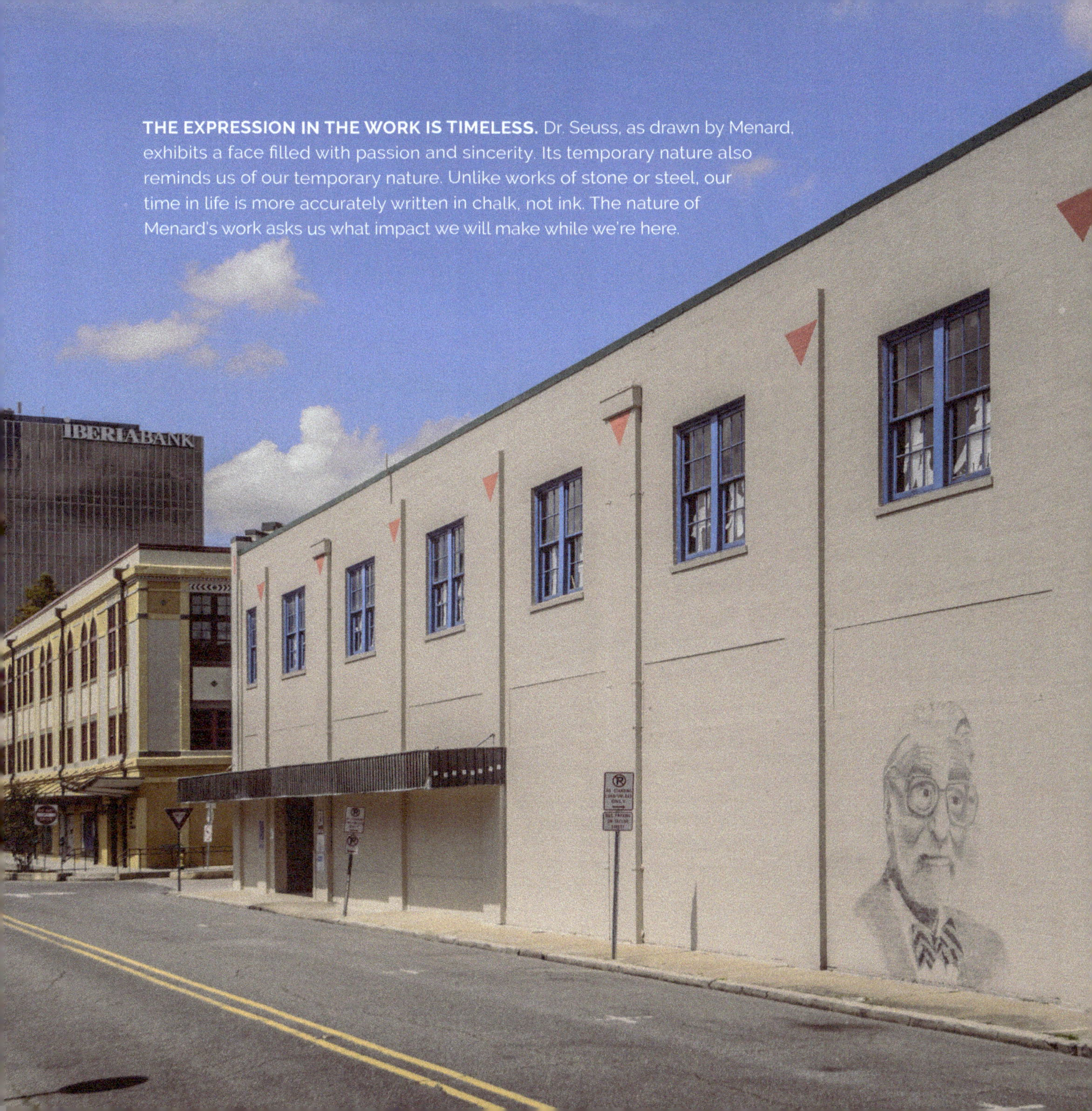

THE EXPRESSION IN THE WORK IS TIMELESS. Dr. Seuss, as drawn by Menard, exhibits a face filled with passion and sincerity. Its temporary nature also reminds us of our temporary nature. Unlike works of stone or steel, our time in life is more accurately written in chalk, not ink. The nature of Menard's work asks us what impact we will make while we're here.

Déjà Vu
Artist: MIKE STANSBURY

IF THE WALLS COULD TALK IN LAFAYETTE CITY HALL THEY'D BE FILLED WITH THE VOICES OF LOCAL ARTISTS. Painting, sketches and sculpture constantly adorn the main lobby area, a space fittingly used for announcements and gatherings. At the center of this space, towering nearly two stories is a carved wooden sculpture called Déjà Vu.

IRONICALLY, THIS IS ONE SCULPTURE YOU PROBABLY HAVEN'T SEEN BEFORE.

Déjà Vu was carved by an artist who traveled an unlikely path to sculpture and public art. His name was Kenneth "Mike" Stansbury.

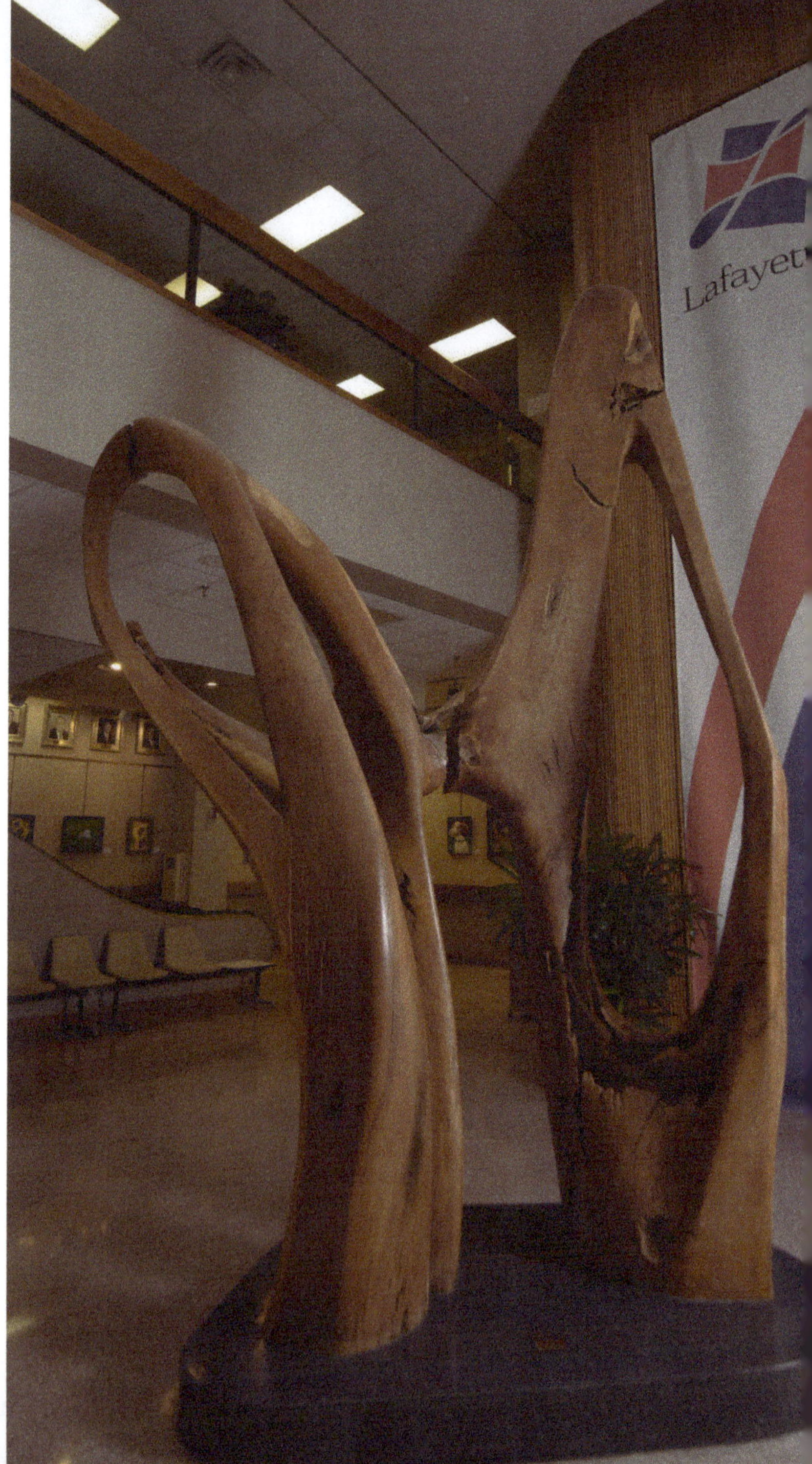

One of his first loves was weightlifting and, like all things in Stansbury's life, he pursued it passionately. Many of his weightlifting legends live on, as does his influence on a number of athletes who competed with and were coached by him. He opened Lafayette's first health club and is recognized by University of Louisiana-Lafayette and the Acadian Museum for his athletic accomplishments, including coaching several local athletes to national titles.

Stansbury's athletic ability outwardly symbolized an inner passion and he focused that passion toward a multitude of vocations. He received national awards for photography including the prestigious NOGI award from the Academy of Underwater Arts & Sciences. He excelled at spear fishing, hunting, bridge and — according to many who knew him — everything he put his mind to.

Stansbury's love of sculpture resulted in a tremendous collection of works. They were often created in conjunction with his wife Andrée and eventually filled their home. Acadiana Center for the Arts hosted the couple's work and the collection filled the facility's largest gallery (with art to spare). He was undoubtedly passionate . . . especially when it came to three trees.

Construction of a new city hall on the site of the former Sears & Roebuck building required a few compromises. The projected size of the new building would require the removal of three large live oaks. Rather than simply see the trees go to firewood, mulch or a landfill, Stansbury turned one of them into a work of art.

At the center of the Lafayette City Hall atrium stands what Robert Dafford[31] calls "the soul" of that tree. Stansbury carved away the bark and whittled into the massive oak, leaving a skeleton bearing the stress marks, hollowed crevices and cracks — scars of the tree's long life — all contrasted by the smooth curves of a more youthful form.

IT'S WORTH BEARING WITNESS TO THIS TREE'S SOUL. And judging by the work's title, it's something Stansbury saw all too often. The sculpture calls to consciousness our community's development efforts in the name of progress and our regrets when there is so little left of our natural spaces.

31 One facet of The City Hall Murals by Dafford pictures the three live oaks in painted archways as a tribute to their existence.

"Lafayette has changed a lot over the years. It used to be very inward looking and self-satisfied, because it was such a fortunate place in many ways, and didn't feel any great need for more ...*Now, things are much more dynamic, connective, growing and positive.* I believe Lafayette's creative community was instrumental in this enhancement, or at the very least, one of the best expressions of it.

The city has a tremendous future, creatively."

— JAMES GARLAND

THE ART OF COMMUNITY

If the recent creative crescendo is any indication of the future, Lafayette is on the verge of an artistic coming-out party. Awards for "Happiest City" in the United States, designation as a top 10 destination for American vacations, twice-awarded status as the "Tastiest Town in the South," and recognition as "One of America's Best Music Towns"[32] (and more) are putting this once relatively-unknown city on the radar of cultural enthusiasts across the country.

Jim Garland's observation mirrors that of Robert Dafford. Both convey that the city, indeed the entire region, possesses an innate sense of creativity rooted in a balanced blend of cultural history and on-the-spot ingenuity. It's only now that the nation is beginning to take notice.

The city, as a collective organism, also intuitively understands something many communities miss, something Wilde might recognize — art reminds us of who we are and points us in the direction of fulfillment in that realization. Lafayette is what happens when the confluence of deep French, African, German, Native American, Spanish, and more recently Vietnamese and Mexican roots meet a cultural expectation of wit, ingenuity and joy. As Garland points out, the city had no need to share this — it was content with these riches on its own. Today, however, the city's vale is lifted.

Rather than react with exclusivity or even feigned embarrassment, the city has opened up. It's as if invitations have gone out to attend what was once a secret party. The festivals grow each year. Chefs gravitate to the scene. And art gains steady ground in galleries, performances and public spaces.

FUELED BY CULTURAL ENCOURAGEMENT, Lafayette's governmental organizations are putting monetary energy behind creative expansion. Dafford's city hall murals are evidence. After nearly two decades of needed exterior maintenance on city hall, the council approved for it not only to be painted but for Dafford's skilled artistry to elevate the site to become a canvas of artistically-rendered stories.

---

32 This is really only a small part of the recognition Lafayette has achieved since 2012. Read the complete list at www.lafayettetravel.com/media/awards.

The University of Louisiana at Lafayette's 2013 master plan includes a dramatic increase in walkability and public spaces (or "outdoor rooms" as they are sometimes called). The university is putting resources behind public art in the process as a way of making these spaces more enjoyable for everyone.

Lafayette's Downtown Development Authority launched its "Creativity Everywhere" campaign as part of its 2014 goal to improve the aesthetic value (and consequent actual value) of public spaces in the downtown district. The result has been an explosion in creative expression in the area including many of the examples described previously.

City-Parish government's 2015 Plan Lafayette initiative engaged countless citizens, challenging them to design the city they wanted to see in 2035 and beyond. One of the final report's first statements emphasizes the town's creative roots and reads, "In 2035, Lafayette is one of the nation's most exceptional communities, renowned for its rich Cajun and Creole heritage, its *creative* scene and culture of innovation, and its authentic 'joie de vivre.'" The report identified "Communicating value of arts, culture, and local history in economic terms" as a clear next step for the community.

And that is where the city seems poised . . . at the threshold between a known and accepted creative past and an economically, investment-worthy creative future. Consider now that four of the works featured here were created in the past year. In short, a match has been lit. The fuel is forthcoming.

The reports and plans attempt to define something invisible but quite tangible about Lafayette's success as a community. That's because a true sense of community requires some sort of group connectedness, an abstract but felt concept. Whether it's through history, pride, triumph, wonder, joy, play or countless other notions, communities exist well beyond a bunch of people living near each other. They are a sense of shared connection.

In the daily shuffle of work, school, dining, dating, children, and chores, **it's human to lose sight of those facets of life that fill our sense of self and connect us with others.**

Beyond giving us opportunities to simply stop and smell the roses, public art can imbue a space with those things that we often miss. It reminds us that our soulfulness comes from our past, our environment and ourselves. It goes well beyond the works themselves to create literal, physical connection points that we can share with one another and with visitors.

Lafayette's sense of connection around public art makes the difference between a good and a great community in dramatic ways the city is now prepared to explore. Residents of Lafayette aren't just looking for a place to live; they want a place to build a life. Public art adds an indispensable ingredient, a thickener of sorts, to that recipe.

Art has always played a role in Lafayette's sense of community, but as our global economy and remote technology gives companies and workers more freedom to choose where to live, it's becoming a more critical factor in economic development. Four years ago, Chattanooga, Tennessee officials reported that Volkswagen's decision to locate a plant there was influenced heavily by their robust arts environment. This year officials from technology companies reported this asset as an influencing factor for choosing Lafayette as a location for expansion.

Four years ago, we began to see governmental groups study returns from public art investments. The Athens Herald reported how the state of Michigan found that every $1 invested in nonprofit arts and cultural groups resulted in more than $51 in economic investment. Lafayette's planning, initiatives began in nearly the same time frame and the dedication of public funds is proof positive that similar phenomena would hold true in this community.

The Lafayette Convention and Visitors Commission has historically leveraged the city's creativity as a travel destination. That strategy is proving to be successful. A Travel Industry Association of America study found that 65% of travelers included a cultural, arts, heritage or historic activity or event while traveling and 32% added extra time to their travel itinerary for this purpose. Most researchers feel that arts and culture will not only remain a prominent influencer of travel decisions, but will grow in importance in the foreseeable future.

Sometimes those economic investments can have more direct returns than expected. Dan Rosenfeld writes in CityLab how developers in Los Angeles invested $75,000 to install murals on the side of a low-income development only to receive millions worth of publicity in return. Another investor coordinated the efforts of a public artist with an architect to achieve striking results — the space was so attractive they received a steady stream of photography and film licensing agreements. The area's steadily growing film scene hints that none of these scenarios are beyond the scope of Lafayette's potential.

The beauty of these studies, initiatives and funding platforms for Lafayette residents is the reassurance that the city has not only been ahead of the curve in areas of arts, culture and community but it is "doubling down" on its creative assets as a critical future success factor. It was always evident in the city's music and food. It was heard at festivals and street fairs. And the cultural energy behind public art still resonates.

Continued initiatives from government agencies and nonprofit museums keep the fires burning but it is the people of this city who originally fanned the flames. These initiatives are a product of a people who love their art. And they're happy to share it with you.

Acknowledgments

IN ADDITION TO THE ARTISTS AND BENEFACTORS MENTIONED IN THIS BOOK I am grateful to have had the help of several people in our community who care deeply about public art's role in our future. To Brittany Broussard, thank you for embracing the lofty concept of living our art. It makes little logical sense at times, but some of the best things in life are completely illogical — glad to ride these waves with you. To Peggy Grace and Abi Augello, my partners at Engle & Völkers Lafayette-Lake Charles, thank you for seeing the importance of this project both for me personally and for our community as a whole. Mary Beyt and Brian Guidry, thank you for your initial guidance, interpretations and honest opinions. You shaped the way I structured this book and how I now interpret all forms of creative expression. LouAnne Greenwald and Laura Blereau, I appreciate your candor and connections. Kelly Strenge and Herman Mhire, thanks for connecting me to some great creative minds. Paige Krauss and the staff at Acadiana Center for the Arts, your inspiration and guidance proved invaluable. Thanks also to Susan Gilette, Renée Roberts, Carlee Alm-Labar, Sarah Berthelot, Amanda Elliott and Elise Bouchner.

Lastly, to Sophie and Jacques . . . when you were both two years of age I began taking you to ArtWalk. I requested that you look at the works of art and ask yourself two simple questions: **1) What do you see?** and **2) How does it make you feel?** Your answers made me laugh, cry and delight in the unexpected possibilities seen only through your eyes. I hope this book offers you deeper enjoyment and understanding of the wonderful art this city has to offer.

Bibliography

Aristotle. Poetics. 335 BC. Google Books (books.google.com)

Caldwell, John R. Public art has positive economic impact. 21 March 2012. 21 11 2016 http://onlineathens.com/opinion/2012-03-21/caldwell-public-art-has-positive-economic-impact

Elliott, Amanda Jean. Throwing the Gauntlet. Periodical. Lafayette: The Independent, 2016

Gould, Philip. The Public Art of Robert Dafford. University of Louisiana at Lafayette, 2014

Jr., Paul F. Stahls. An Acadian Journey. March 2008. November 2016 http://www.myneworleans.com/Louisiana-Life/Spring-2008/An-Acadian-Journey/

LaVergne, Al. Albert LaVergne: Vision in Metal. 2012. 21 11 2016 http://allavergne.com/

Longfellow, Henry Wadsworth. Evangeline: A tale of Acadie. http://www.hwlongfellow.org/works_evangeline.shtml

Pierce, Walter. "'Tongue' in groove: Salvaged sculpture installed downtown." The Independent 28 August 2009

Plato. The Republic. 380 BC. 21 November 2016 (books.google.com)

Project for Public Spaces. How Art Economically Benefits Cities. 1 January 2009. 21 November 2016 http://www.pps.org/blog/how-art-economically-benefits-cities/

Rodrigue, Wendy. Musings of an Artist's Wife. 10 November 2009. November 2016 http://www.wendyrodrigue.com/2009/11/there-are-enough-rodrigue-evangelines.html

Wiggs, Robert. Wiggs Polysutures. 2006. November 2016 http://wiggspolysutures.com/

Civic Initiatives

Downtown Lafayette Action Plan
http://www.lafayettela.gov/comprehensiveplan/documents/downtown_action_plan_web.pdf

University of Louisiana-Lafayette Master Plan
http://louisiana.edu/sites/louisiana/files/DesignVision_ULMPrevised9.3.14-small.pdf

City of Lafayette Master Plan
http://planlafayette.com/assets/Version_CPCAC_Final.pdf

Acadiana Center for the Arts and LEDA's ArtSpark Grants
http://www.acadianacenterforthearts.org/artspark

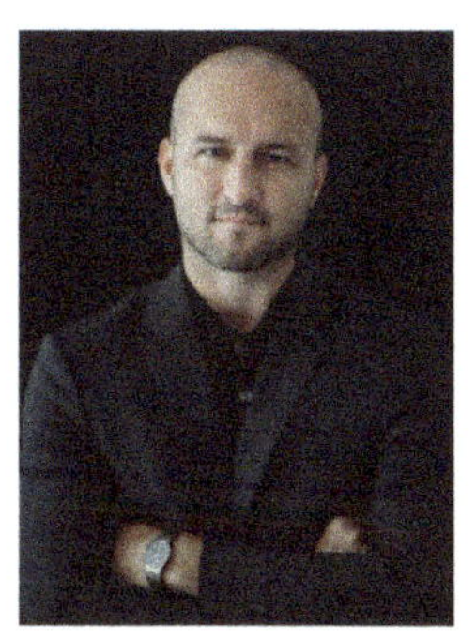

Author Jeremy C. Broussard has called Lafayette, Louisiana his home since 1996. His pursuits have often captured the unique spirit of Acadiana's blended heritage and passionate way of life, focusing largely on projects aimed at history and improving the community at large. Broussard's written work spans a range of award-winning commercial projects including speeches, television commercials, multimedia experiences and more. He is the executive producer of the documentary film *Little Houses: A short film about death.* and author of the subsequent book *Grave House Legends*. Broussard co-authored the business book *The Nexus Initiative* with his mentor Brent Henley. More information about Broussard's work can be found at JeremyCBroussard.com.

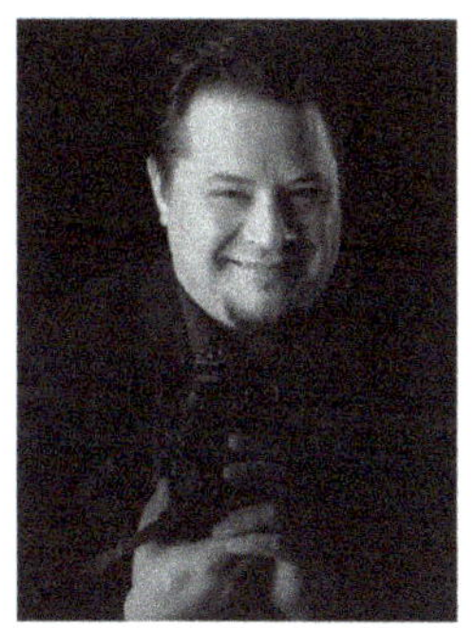

Photographer Travis Gauthier is a native of Lafayette, Louisiana. He is a graduate of The Art Institute of Houston where he earned an Associate of Applied Science in Photography. With over twenty years experience in several different photographic arenas; from photojournalism, to retouching, lab work, to the portrait and wedding industry, Travis has made photography a lifelong avocation. Travis enjoys cycling, vinyl record collecting, current events, pop culture, and cinema. Learn more about Gauthier's photography at ZoomPhotoStudio.com.

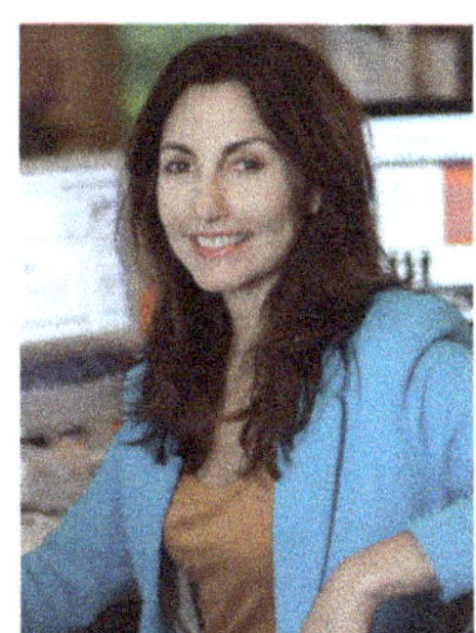

Designer Elizabeth Bell Landry believes commercial design should never say, 'Look at me' but rather, 'Look at this' — a philosophy that has underpinned her approach to design for more than two decades. Her experience at Peter A. Mayer, The Graham Group, McIlhenny Company (makers of world famous Tabasco®) and UL Lafayette in positions as international services coordinator, art director, designer and editor garnered the designer numerous awards from Acadiana Advertising Federation and the New Orleans Art Directors and Designers Association. As the owner of eBellDesign in Downtown Lafayette, Elizabeth specializes in brand development, print advertising, promotional collateral pieces, point-of-purchase displays, in-store graphics, direct mail, custom publishing and electronic marketing.

Experience Lafayette's Public Art

Public art continues to grow in Lafayette and there's no experience quite like seeing it in person. Information including apps, maps and coordinates for Lafayette's public art can be found at the book's website: **ArtofthePeople.net**

Support for this book comes from the Acadiana Center for the Arts (ACA), Lafayette Economic Development Authority (LEDA) and Acadiana Economic Development with additional support from the Lafayette Convention and Visitors Commission (Lafayette Travel). These organizations not only promote local art as a source of enjoyment but also recognize creativity as one of Lafayette's core economic assets. These local art advocates make Lafayette a continuously attractive and interesting place to live. Thank you for your vision.

www.ingramcontent.com/pod-product-compliance
Lightning Source LLC
LaVergne TN
LVHW060628110826
845147LV00015B/962

* 9 7 8 0 9 8 2 9 2 3 9 6 2 *